SELF-DISCOVERY
from
FIRST PRINCIPLES

SELF-DISCOVERY *from* FIRST PRINCIPLES

KRISHNA KUMAR

PARTRIDGE
A Penguin Company

Partridge books may be ordered through booksellers or by contacting:

Partridge India
Penguin Books India Pvt.Ltd
11, Community Centre, Panchsheel Park, New Delhi 110017
India
www.partridgepublishing.com
Phone: 000.800.10062.62

CONTENTS

Dedicated To

The co-author who does not wish to reveal her name

PREFACE

The book fulfils a heartfelt desire to share my observations on self-discovery. In explaining this natural process, I do not lean on any schools of religion, philosophy or psychology. This book has been in the making for many years, and this venture became possible only through my collaboration with the co-author. Since she and I live in different places now, ours was mainly an epistolary relationship in developing this work. Earlier, our disquisitions on almost everything under the Sun have enabled us to link self-discovery with everyday experiences.

The quest for self-realisation took us on many paths to quench our angst. Right from meditating in the mountains and sea shore or in contemplating the essence of various spiritual texts, our tenacity took the better part of our lives in this labile journey. Temples and mantras, sojourns with masters, and discussions on reality made us seek the unknown. It has enriched both our lives remarkably well. We can now remember our immature and often insane lives before this change of heart happened. The world around us has not changed much, but there is indescribable peace and satisfaction within.

Meenama was an inspiration to many who had come in contact with her. She is my mother and through her sacrifice and wishes the quest for knowledge found fruition. Carnatic Music too had a special part which gave me scope for introspection. I wish to thank KM, who encouraged me to be in awareness and made my life delectable in the pursuit of self-discovery. *"EndarO mahAnubhAvu-landariki vandanamu."* This is a popular composition by the legendary Sri Thyagaraja, which means, "salutation to all the great ones."

In fact, the whole cosmos has acted as a trigger, for self-discovery. After years of haggling with various ideas, my bloated ego burst. The umbilical cord connecting the unknown with my conditioning got severed. What remains is the freedom to observe without any constraints. There is witnessing of the constant flow of phantasmagoria of events, things, people and culture in the world. In focusing attention on the known one can celebrate existence and, there is immediacy in sharing this with everyone.

I disclaim any divine proximity or esoteric wisdom spurting out from me that can elevate the readers to a higher level of spiritual intoxication. I do not delineate a path for the seekers who work toward a goal. There are of course, pointers that may trigger urgency in the readers to look at everything, including, their own selves objectively. The book caters to serious seekers of enlightenment, as well as, for those who want to bring out the best in them.

I welcome you wholeheartedly to go through the book and celebrate your presence in the world. All living and non-living things are expression and part of the universe. Everyone has a choice for self-discovery. By doing so, each of us can lead a tranquil and purposeful life in understanding. It will bring to the fore our innate potential, and remove any blocks within us.

Finally, freedom has wings. It reaches out to everything everywhere and everyone with whom one comes across. The process of sharing this awareness to others will be effortless.

INTRODUCTION

The book traces the origin and organisation of life on earth. The story extends right from the Big bang to the present world of humans. In this history, several species have evolved and disappeared. The universe itself provides all the ingredients to create any life form. There are bare necessities that are required to evolve certain traits in all living beings. Even a slight change in the natural parameters could upset the continuation of life on earth.

The human organism is the body housing the consciousness with its many mental faculties. The word organism is just to emphasise the similarity of humans with other animals. In terms of manifesting life using elements in nature, there is equality in the process of creation. Humans have self-awareness and uniqueness. They also have their impressions, which are knowledge, experience and conditioning to interact in the world. Discovering one's physical and mental faculties is aligning with the known.

The collective wisdom immanent in society has a strong influence on individuals. The individuals integrate with society, and form institutions that power the world. The dynamic between an individual and society is complex. People can see their conditioning by introspecting on the ties with society, as well. When people chase an unknown figment of their imagination, their behaviour is but the conditioning in a reactionary mode. Embracing the known brings clarity and equanimity. Engagement with the world will then be an objective response in any situation.

For many millennia, people have believed that god-realisation is a means to touch upon the source of creation itself. Godmen have made a profound influence in the world by declaring their proximity to the unknown. Self-discovery is also in understanding the conditioning that make a person anchor on to such claims. The declaration of such realisation is only an idea which has, however, become part of human conditioning. Each and every person in the world has a choice to a life in discovery and joy. Self-discovery is not an esoteric idea like a mirage in the desert. On the contrary, it is a dynamic and expressible function, totally in tune with the known.

13.8: THE STORY OF LIFE

*H*uman lifespan is around hundred years. The latest scientific estimates suggest that the story of life began 13.8 billion years ago. There are connections between these two disparate events and time scales. One needs to acknowledge that the universe is the only home, and none can ever leave it. The angst is in wanting to return to an imaginary one. The elements of the universe are indispensable for the evolution of any life form; humans included. There has been a continuous link with the DNA or biological building blocks of many previous life forms that have manifested on earth. There are links both gross and subtle that one can never sever with anything at all in nature.

Life as people know it did not begin with humans and in all likelihood may not end with that species either. Human life is one of the wonders of existence in its many majestic forms. There is a mystery in the story which unfolds within an epic of the cosmos right alongside it. Humans straddle the trajectories of both the individual and the universal evolution unconsciously. Self-discovery jolts one up to the awareness that any individual story of life started 13.8 billion years ago.

The Origins

Children are fond of bed-time stories. The tales open up the doors of the young minds to a fantasy-land and softly lull them to sleep. There are many such narrations on human origins recounted by men in places far, far away and long, long ago. Grandmothers picked them up from their grandmothers and children all over the world grew up on hearing these fascinating accounts of creation. They are colourful and naturally fire the imagination of the listeners.

Humanity went to deep sleep with these schemes in mind and has been dreaming since then. Last century, someone woke up people and told something with a twist in the story-line. He said it all started with a big bang. The very mention of such a loud blast interrupted the sleep of some, and they began searching for the source again in their sleep. The others dozed off carrying yet another plot for animating their dreams.

This partly explains why a new tribe has emerged, which wants to cross both the streams and intelligently design a fresh form for their ideas. People will snooze, for there is no reason to be awake. The origin is waiting at dawn, in the morrow, when all of humanity will rise from this slumber.

Life begets observation. Knowledge arises from observation, and it helps us learn everything about life. Naturally, the proper study of life gravitates in knowing its own origin. This finds resonance in the research of scientists and the speculations of philosophers alike. Scratch a little on history and human ancestry becomes nebulous as one goes back in time. So many species preceded Homo sapiens in evolution. Perhaps unicellular organisms are the ones one needs to recognise as the progenitors of all life on earth. Well before the appearance of life on the planet only matter, energy and space-time materialised in the universe. Further back in time all claims of one's origin could purely have been the potentiality of creation; beyond which one hits a wall.

Everything born is a mix and mash of its parents' genes propelled by evolutionary impulses. It is natural to seek one's roots to identify with one's origin. In fact, everyone connects with one's own parents, grandparents and so on to feel part of the family tree. Family faithfully creates lineage, cemented by culture and reinforced by religion. For all practical purposes, most people can trace their ancestry to only a few generations back. Nevertheless, the human mind seems to swear by an unshakeable identity with tribes, religions, race or nationality as if they were here since eternity.

Only with time did the things, one sees around evolve and develop into animate and inanimate entities. Does anyone inherit a chart of evolution? Even nature seems to be oblivious of any blueprint and works incessantly not revealing an inkling of the future. For her, there is no future or past. The present is only a state observable in this form. In quantum levels even observation could alter events. It is doubtful if observing the universe right now holds any bearing on its future.

Any observer perceives the observation as a true record of reality. One is only witness to situations and can in no way vouch for one's future predicament or that of the universe. There have been countless life forms, including humans, dinosaurs, fish and cellular organisms that flourished on earth. No creature could have imagined that it is indeed evolving to become what is in the present. All are creatures of circumstances able to witness a slice of the universe with their faculties.

None is in the driver's seat. There is no driver or map which one is aware of. There is no goal post to reach either. One has the capability to watch the drama of life flow every moment. One neither knows the origin nor any destination. In simple terms, this is the human experience. Let there be patience and knowledge to look at oneself and make the best out of one's own strengths. It is imperative to wear clarity as one's badge to create a sensible lifestyle for one and all. Both the environment and people count in this regard. There is nothing else one can do except to celebrate life in observation and action.

Humans are certainly curious by nature. It shows up in the way the ideas of creation have cropped up in all lands and peoples at all times. In modern times, science is hope for many to go to the root of how one belongs here. Even today both creation myths and Big bang theory coexist to fill the gaps to understand the origin of the universe. All these ideas are but a continual flow of human expression in the quest for the realisation of one's place in the planet.

The Creation Myths

If an event were to occur in say, ten minutes or even ten years one can try to be part of the same. In the formation of the universe and its subsequent evolution though, no one can be a witness; one can only imagine it based on the result of investigations. Ancient ancestors might have imagined causes for the basic questions of life based on their own observations and conjectures. No wonder there are several wonderful stories on creation. Many people still hold on to one of these myths as part of their religious text and vouch for its veracity.

Fortunately, there are no abrupt cataclysmic changes happening to earth's immediate surroundings in the cosmos now. Instead, there is a steady state of order and harmony in nature that allows survival and observation of the same. The time-slice of human life span is of infinitesimal proportions compared to the billions of years for the universe. Any knowledge on the evolution of the universe can only be hearsay and can never be firsthand experience. The curiosity impels the researchers to turn every stone to break the code of existence. Research on things from outer space to biological cells has enriched lives. The results encourage scientists to embark on many fruitful journeys of discovery. Many a puzzle remains; not to mention the phenomenon of consciousness that is yet to be understood in the context of creation.

Any healthy human has the logical intelligence and of course awareness to ferret out information to try to get to the core of one's being. Nevertheless, there is an inherent limitation imposed on one's ability. From scientific studies, one thing is clear; the universe did not come along with the existing life forms during its inception. Life forms are only a consequence of many processes in the universe. No one can go back in time and participate with the forces that created all this. That would imply one to create oneself along with the universe, which is absurd. All the knowledge one acquires can at best feed on to one's sense of wonder and awe of the nature of creation.

Scientists may claim an atomic chamber is a laboratory for studying a mini Sun, and a collider may throw light on the creation of fundamental particles. There is no doubt about the work or results of such grand experiments that answer the 'what and how' of physical forces. The very fundamental question as to the 'why' of nature still remains baffling. In other words, the original reason is elusive to grasp.

To resolve this existential issue, the religious elite has ascribed the glory to a figurehead called god and made him responsible for bringing forth the universe, humans and other creatures. There is another group, which says that the life force or the potentiality has always been extant. For them, life expresses in different ways and one is witness to the current possibility. All the seeking and research need to confront this eternal conundrum.

It will be fair enough to admit the ignorance of the primal cause. By all means let scientific research continue with full force and vigour; it may open up peep-holes along the way for us to know more about life. In the same breath let us realise that, with the present faculties of cognition and knowledge, it is impossible to know what the mind desires to uncover. There is no key that opens the vault of secrets. Some so-called realised claimants may swear by their omniscience, yet they have no clue to communicate the secrets of the universe. Either way the pursuit or imagination of a realm beyond one's ken is futile. What best one can do to make life on the planet bearable if not enjoyable is to know one's own self well and organise society better.

This is not a defeatist attitude at all, but a realistic one to live life in fullness. Understanding brings home the vanity of ego in falsely nurturing delusions like the supremacy of one's abilities. Many do believe that even if they cannot dive into the unknown; their gurus, prophets, or saviours speak the voice of the almighty. Faith pulls the flock together and makes them lead their lives and societies according to the uttering of these realised people. The seekers try to touch the current of life through various practices and sacrifices. Somehow when there is unshakeable certainty of the futility in the very quest itself, there is tremendous peace and cheer in the movement of life.

The Scientific theories

Scientists have confirmed with certainty that the universe got formed 13.8 billion years ago as a result of the Big bang. What does that physically mean to grapple with such a large number? Practically, it is difficult to conceive of such a spread of time because one is not witness to its making. Scientists can only do a logical study to know the origin. The period in question seems like infinity to the earthlings who can at best aspire to make it a century. The universe started cooling down after its formation. From the fiery inferno galaxies, stars and other celestial objects materialised.

The good earth seems to be five billion years old. The same story got repeated, and the planet cooled down to support an environment that is conducive to life. It was a case of matter, matter everywhere, but not a soul to see. Later on, something stirred up to make a unique product the earth is going to witness—a single-cell organism. It moves; exchanges energy and strangely replicates. Life abounds on the planet. Earth, now, teems with millions of life forms. There are fishes in the sea, animals and plants on land and birds in the sky. During this fantastic evolution, there were mass extinctions of several species due to many geological and other reasons. Newer life forms emerged from the ashes of the previous catastrophic destructions. Humans have finally arrived.

When it comes to the origin of life and all the necessities like matter and energy, one is in the dark. It is mind-boggling to measure the quantity of energy in the entire universe. Law of conservation of energy states that: energy can neither be created nor be destroyed. In that situation can one assume the law is applicable even before the Big bang? The same goes to life, as well. Life only begets life. Does that imply life existing prior to the Big bang? Space-time and other fundamental physical quantities are still mysteries—riddles wrapped in an enigma.

To explain many phenomena, it is necessary to assume the creation of such basics along with the birth of the universe. That event is spectacularly important in the timeline of scientific consciousness. There is no way for anyone to preside over a meaningful conclusion on these unknowable questions. What one can do at best is to be aware of the present knowledge and experience.

One can see many favourable patterns in nature, both fixed and cyclic that has made one organise life on earth. The ground rarely gives way, and similarly, the seas seldom breach their boundary. The immutable circadian rhythms and predictable monsoon patterns are examples of cyclical patterns in nature that are the basis for existence.

The Necessities

The necessities are the many ifs and buts for life to appear on earth. These are important to all beings for their own survival. One cannot eliminate any of the necessities to live in isolation either. In a way, everything is part and parcel of the universe itself and vice versa. All beings are singularities with consciousness able to know a few scenes that they sense. In addition to this, one can manipulate and match patterns here and there to reassemble what already exists. In this process, humans have played enough with the environment to the point of its destruction. Now, there is a need to be very careful in leaving the necessities intact for all the future generations to come.

Any organism can exist only in an environment that supports certain basic necessities. Even if, one of these things is absent, life as people know it cannot happen. Space-time is the most essential parameter for life to appear. Energy comes next and pervades the universe. Matter is the building block for any organism to take shape. Encoding and decoding signals create information which living being use for their survival. Awareness makes intelligence perceptible, and any life form tick. Nothing is absolute, and they all relate to each other.

The universe holds the fundamental necessities for any life form to sustain. One observation that does not miss the eye is that, evolution has taken in all the elements from the environment to create life. There is nothing in any being to suggest something extraneous to earth, as part of its biology. Living beings are all products of, live in and finally merge back to the same elements they come from the earth. They are indeed the universe.

Space and Time

Space-time manifestation has allowed all the cosmic dramas to be enacted and strangely it lets conscious beings witness the same, as well. Can anyone ever think of taking one's own self out of the universe? It is unimaginable and akin to cessation of life itself. Isolating the self from the grandeur of space-time is nothing short of constricting one's own existential experiencing. Therefore, the life-principle is part of and one with the universe.

The vast universe is like a four-dimensional giant screen. It has three dimensions of space and one that of time, which hold the earth and other bodies in their orbit. Movement lets one explore space and time. Life needs movement in some form or the other. Even plants and animals move in all the three dimensions. Humans have also evolved adjusting to this law. The space-time matrix provides every being the opportunity to be born, live and die in its arms.

The brain feels the scope of space as much as the depths of time. Unlike space, time is unidirectional and irreversible; the arrow of time goes only from the past to the future. The faculty of awareness enables one to bank on memory, witness change and feel the flow of time gliding from moment to moment in one's lives. In essence, there are a lot of processes, which bring the sense of time to one's consciousness. This understanding reinforces the centrality of the organism in experiencing all that one is aware of including time. As noted earlier regarding space, time too has its origin with the Big bang. The remarkable thing is the ability of consciousness to perceive both space and time. Everything is indeed a product of space-time, both literally and figuratively.

Energy

Energy is fundamental to life, and its inflow and outflow happen all the time. Energy interchange happens from the atomic to cosmic levels. The Sun is the primary source of all the planetary energy needs. Living things expend energy through movement. Physicists have defined it as the capacity to do work. All life forms get energised by the food they ingest. Any imbalance of energy leads to the living being's discomfort or even death. All living things need to be, therefore, in that energy-band which does not affect the organism adversely.

Matter or Form

The universe contains matter spread across its length and breadth; some of which one can see and feel. The earth on which people live is matter. Matter exists in the form of solid, liquid, gas or even plasma. The atmosphere is gaseous. Rivers, oceans and other water bodies are liquid in form. The rest is solid. The sacredness of matter need not be emphasised more as all life forms make earth their home.

All living entities, including animals and plants have form and shape. Matter is sacrosanct for one to feel life. Living beings depend on food and other basic necessities of life-like air and water, which are all different forms of matter. People rearrange matter endlessly to survive. Life forms breathe matter either as air or water. Atoms and molecules are the fundamental units of matter. They are uniform and do not exhibit variation in their basic characteristics. In the material world, elements are the same in texture, composition and properties. For instance, carbon can never be changed in its purest form, whether in Earth or a distant galaxy. Matter is a building block of the universe.

Signals

All living entities live in a sea of signals or vibrations that can carry information. Without them, life will be unthinkable. The *umwelt* in which organisms live provides a slice of objective reality to it. All these result, thanks to the processing ability in all life forms. They turn the many signals they receive and transmit into information. Each species adapts to situations using signals and intelligence. For instance, humans can be cognisant of a band of the electromagnetic spectrum, whereas bats rely on a different band for constructing their objective world.

Technology may bring one closer to the wonders of the things in the cosmic scale or the atomic scale that one cannot perceive with the given senses. The instruments collect signals and normalise them for human cognition. This is the gift of knowledge one gets thanks to the universality of signals even from far and wide.

Environment

All beings require a suitable environment to form and sustain. The slightest variation in any of the constituent parameters will make the environment inhospitable. For instance, even if the atmospheric temperature rises by a few degrees life will become extinct; as happened to the dinosaurs. There is tremendous interdependence among humans, animals, plants and even matter on the planet. The delicate balance needs to be maintained, and ecology protected so that all species may thrive freely on earth.

Awareness

Awareness means many things to many people, and a clear and definitive interpretation eludes scientists. Sans it, no living being would experience the world. One does not know if this greatest leap in evolution is just an epiphenomenon or an independent occurrence. From observations, though, one can safely allude it to cognise all the contents, processes and abilities of the mind. Perception of the past, present and future as functions of time, memory, intelligence, emotions and other mental faculties are all part of consciousness.

All life forms exhibit awareness in varying stages of maturity. Humans probably top the list, and other species have it in lesser degrees. Self-awareness arises with life. Humans are conscious of their own self-awareness. Attention, when it turns on itself, brings focus to the underlying consciousness one possesses.

Awareness cannot be isolated from the body of any organism. It is part and parcel of the body and nervous system in particular. Defects in the brain attest to this fact; people with various problems of the brain exhibit abnormal symptoms and aberrations in behaviour. Psychedelic substances can alter perceptions of reality. They open the doors to subconscious storage of knowledge. Neurosciences offer plenty of scope for further research and study of this enigmatic segment of living beings. Consciousness above all creates a distinction between lifeless matter and life.

THE NATURE

Is nature absolute? There is mystery everywhere, which forces people to hold on to even a straw as security outside of them. An idea of the absolute would help to tide over the uncertainties they face every moment in life. This unresolved vulnerability adds spice and magic to life. The nature and the necessities of life seem to take pretty much the scope of non-negotiable parameters for existence.

The current state of the cosmos is right in the middle of a long and unchartered evolutionary journey, neither present in the beginning nor at the finale. No one can claim to be the creators; all are witnesses of their lives and the world.

Cataclysmic events occur naturally in the universe. Asteroids pulverising planets or black holes swallowing up even massive stars are common phenomena. However, it is unnatural for anyone to resort to mental, physical and behavioural violence, but it happens all the time. Non-violence becomes effortless when one realises one's true nature and acts accordingly. Self-discovery is the harbinger of harmony within oneself and the world.

There are certain commonalities regarding the way all living beings function. Movement lets any organism conquer the space-time matrix. Communication happens again through movement for information processing. There are various modes of existence like waking and non-waking states. All life forms have basic survival instinct. When they reproduce their young ones show differences and variability from them. All beings have a unique identity at birth. Finally, death is common to all living things.

Movement

Life is synonymous with movement. Space-time gets cognized, and communication is possible due to the movement of bodies. The atoms and the subatomic particles too are in motion at great speeds. These vibrations are the building blocks of reality as one perceives it. Movement is the quintessence of all the signals generated. The scope of frequencies in defining matter, energy and information, is truly amazing.

Sound, which includes music and speech, is a set of frequencies. Every shade of colour has a frequency associated with it. The same applies to other sense organs, as well. All these sensory inputs are data in the form of electrical signals. They vibrate at certain frequencies. The instruments that capture these vibrations are the sense organs, and the one that decodes all these inputs is the brain. Movement produces all sensations. Breathing too is about movement of air. Thoughts are vibrations and can be studied using machines which analyse the frequency spectrum of the brain signals. People have seen how matter, sensations, breath, bodily activities and even mental processes are all movements.

Metaphorically, one can compare anything with a wave which rides on the ocean. It makes sense if one decomposes the object and the world as waves of frequencies dancing all around. In the constant flux, there is a silent realisation of all the movement happening around the witness.

States

There are many states of consciousness expressed by all living beings at any point of time in their lives. In humans, they are the waking, sleeping, dreaming, deep sleep and unconscious states. It is difficult to know if animals have similar tendencies as humans do. Humans are active by day, and they rest at night. Some animals are nocturnal. There is a deep connection between all organisms and their environment. Over millennia, living beings have developed innate capabilities to survive. The different states of consciousness are fascinating phenomena that have evolved over millions of years.

All the planning, conscious actions, emotions, logic and, in fact, the full force of consciousness that one makes, comes into effect only during the waking state. The organism need not be in active mode all the time. It needs rejuvenation for which it goes to sleep. During sleep, the body and also part of the consciousness gets deactivated. Dreams kick in to reveal that there is a whole wide world of unconscious field within human beings. The ego is still intact and recognises itself being active. Anaesthesia can create deep states of unconsciousness leaving nothing in memory after one wakes up. Psychedelic substances, as well, create altered states of consciousness.

There is tremendous peace and well being if there is good waking and sleep states in any organism. Any impairment is a wake-up call for introspection. Substance-abuse, sleep deprivation and hyper-activity, are a few things that can be got over by realising the need to be more responsible in one's life. As age progresses, sleep time gets drastically altered. It is then all the more significant to realise the need to keep the mind calm and the body supple when deprived of sleep.

Survival

Survival is for both the self and the species. The birth of any organism brings with it, the survival instinct to counter decay or death. Identification and interdependence are two principal keys one needs to be aware of in this context. For humans, skills, faculties, various internal processes and collective societal regulations are all handy to make them adaptable to changing situations.

Reproduction

Variability

Reproduction guarantees the life of species. Without this remarkable mechanism, there would not have been evolution and so many living beings extant in the planet. Offspring are not identical copies of the parents. They look and feel different. Otherwise, the whole world might look alike. Divergence of characteristics of children from the parents comes about naturally through reproduction. When life gets inspirited into matter, there is variability among the offspring produced. It is said that even two leaves are not alike. Humans are bulkier, taller or fairer from each other. It is interesting to note that, unlike the dry monotony of matter, life is about differences. Life spawns variability. Evolution happens step by step with these differences taking the apt change suitable for the environment.

Gender

Man and woman are biologically different. However, the life force is the same despite their gender difference. For creating life, though, both male and female of the species need to unite. It is in a way a clever strategy for division of labour between the sexes. Probably, it would be too much for a uni-gendered creature to carry on the burden of evolution through asexual reproduction.

Physiological compartmentalisation alone will not suffice to explain away gender. There is a fascinating aspect of cross-sexuality too that occurs in both genders. For instance, a woman may be harbouring male traits and vice versa. Conditioning makes one see gender as either black or white. In fact, there are different shades of gray in between, the duality of the sexes. Even though, the percentage of such people is particularly low, it is an eye-opener to know one's body better.

Gender identity develops due to many reasons. Physical, psychological, cultural and behavioural aspects define one's nature. Role based living plays a crucial role in one's conditioning of how a male or a female ought to live in a society. In objective living, the rigid identification sinks, and the spirit of a shared reason and purpose of one's existence emerges. It renders gender inequality history. Relationship between man and woman then takes on a different meaning.

Sexuality

The bodily and emotional pull for pleasure is overwhelming in all life forms. Just like it is common to avoid pain, one way of satiating the demand for pleasure consummates in the bonding of the male and female forms. Sexuality is at once a physical and psychological nature of the organism. The bait for sex is not only procreation but also the drive for seeking sensations. It involves all the five senses in addition the mind in fulfilling its objective. Once the job is done, the role of man is over. Physically, the role of the male in the process of reproduction is only in the act of sex. The female continues with the procreation through pregnancy and uses her body as the canvas to complete the picture. It takes months and even years to make the offspring stand on its own.

There is a natural attraction between the sexes. Nevertheless, one cannot generalise the same. Homosexuality is also a characteristic of a sizeable population of the species. Gender role-playing is significant in this manifestation. Even though, reproduction as a process is absent in such bonding, sexuality is present in a truly conspicuous manner.

Motherhood

For males, who form half of humanity, motherhood can only be an idea which is daunting. On the contrary, for the mother it is a welcome responsibility. She never disappears and is part and parcel of the child for a much longer time for the creative process to complete. The umbilical cord that connects the mother and the baby continues virtually even after child birth. The baby is dependent on the mother's milk for its sustenance. The mother instinctively bonds physically to her child until it can be safely weaned away from her.

In fact, the actual delivery of any child involves moving life from the formless to a form. However fragile, the process might be it can happen only in the body of the mother. The seed by itself cannot grow without this space and time. In a way, it is akin to the entire universe that has sprouted from the formless during the Big bang. The spirit is the same in any creation, be it the universe, man, animals or even plants and insects. The body's memory is remarkable as it has links to mind, as well. Today's child will be tomorrow's parent.

Creation is an amazing event. As long as the mind tries to control and possess it, there is sorrow. In full understanding, there is a joy in the union of knowledge and experience to adapt to the present which is nothing but the manifestation of creation.

Uniqueness

Nature loves diversity, and it is indeed the spice of life. Each organism is unique. Even cloned animals may have slight differences between them. Individuals are singularities of consciousness in their respective forms. What the body has been doing since the dawn of life on earth is the celebration of its uniqueness. Each organism carries its own identity—its shape. The bodily expression of individuality is awe inspiring. One needs to be proud of one's body and not try to be in someone else's shoes. Self-discovery will subtly make one engage with the world with neither inferiority nor superiority in one's minds.

Realisation of the uniqueness of the form will truly liberate one from any stress to even out differences in the world.

Death

In physical terms, death is the grand culmination of existence. The body disintegrates back to the elements. Once consciousness dips, there is no way one can experience death. The organism shuns it due to the survival instinct it has painstakingly evolved over millions of years. Nevertheless, every entity gets a reward of death at an unknown time. Psychologically, the final parting will always remain a mystery for the dying and sorrow for the dear ones who outlive them. The fear of the unknown, survival instinct, pain and suffering, make death a very compelling reason for introspection.

1: THE HUMAN ORGANISM

*L*et us assume that scientists develop an artificial being in a lab. They engineer all the faculties and functions normal humans have in the cyborg, Org for short. Org has learning and memory abilities too, which allows it to hold many scripts. Except for the makers, it is indistinguishable from a human being for the rest of the population. The desired perfection is the bonus achieved in its shape, abilities, demeanour and responsibility to society. Org has become the de-facto model for anyone to look up to emulate. Does one want the world to be filled with seven billion people living optimally according to a plan the engineers designed for Org? It may be scary indeed for the silent majority, but there could be support for it from a forceful minority.

Self-discovery, no doubt helps one to understand one's style better so as to function more effectively in the world. At the same time, one should not forget that everyone is unique not only in form but also in content. An individual's expressions of living too can be infinitely varied. The number '1' in the heading stands for one's uniqueness in identity. In fact, the very idea of knowing the human organism itself is to create a platform for persons to be their true selves and live accordingly. It is not to turn one into an ideal being. Culture and society, on the contrary, have assiduously popularised it as a virtue. To cut the story short, it is not for others to dictate what one does with one's life. People can then live in freedom and understanding.

The Form

Can one exist without a body? Even if, one imagines oneself as a formless entity, there is still the mind which is nothing but a consequence of one's physical nature. Living beings assume a shape when they are alive. It is no wonder that one shudders to think of passing into formlessness, non-existence or death. In the first place, it is even inconceivable to erase one's own image from one's consciousness. Secondly, if one were to delete consciousness too from the system; it becomes unacceptable. All speculations of the void, soul and other such dimensions are nothing but the mind trying hard to mimic life after death. It wants reassurance in them when it is no more. The known, however, is the body which one can sense in all its glory now.

The intrinsic wealth one carries all the time is one's own body. The gross form pertains to the body, sense organs and breathing. It gives the uniqueness and tools for people to observe themselves and the universe. The human organism operates in space and time. The body with its limbs makes movement through space possible. The mind, which holds the consciousness, perceives time. Animate and inanimate things are indeed products of space-time. Apart from the ability to move, one possesses the ability to communicate, as well. It is the result of both the body and the mind working in tandem with an objective to exchange information. Data flow is a function of time during delivery and reception.

The physical body gives shape to the form, and the virtual body or the mind has developed various faculties. The form hosts the five sense organs, and thanks to them the world is discernible. These organs are the gateways to collect various types of signals, which are omnipresent all the time. They faithfully transfer signals to the brain for processing. The data set could be energy packets in the form of kinetic, light or sound waves. They could also be chemical in nature. Finally, the brain converts these sensory inputs into electrical signals for processing. There is a magic that happens with awareness that aids in perception. The signals tell the story of the universe, and the perceivers can enjoy it and make personal stories in their heads. That is the world one creates in one's brains.

Without the bodies, there is no question of reproduction. The body also allows all types of matter interchange to occur between it and the environment. That includes, air and food for its upkeep. Breathing makes one realise the dependence on air from birth to death. There is a connection between the physical being and the surroundings every moment.

As a thought experiment, imagine cutting off all the five senses one by one. Watch the individual identity transforming. Is it a bundle of memories; and if that too fades away is it nothing but a mass of flesh? Now bring the senses back to life and realise their value in one's existence. The physical body is a marvel of evolution, which has not yet revealed all its secrets. The form gets conceived as an embryo and after birth, grows into an adult, ages on its own and dies without a choice.

The Faculties

Why does one need different mental functions? In relative terms compared to lower life forms, humans have superior gray matter. It has certainly helped the species survive better. As a result, people have more knowledge and comfortable living choices. Another advantage is the cumulative effect of intelligence or the power of the collective wisdom. One can still be greedy and want more abilities to know everything about the self and the universe. To confound matters, some people avow that, in fact, they know something more than what everyone normally experiences. The majority love to believe them, even if they cannot produce any shred of evidence, which support their claim. The wonder of wonders is, people simply are what they are and know what they know; nothing more, nothing less. Assume for the sake of argument that one gets the answers for all one's questions. Open up now, what is one going to do with those incredible answers?

The unseen part of the organism, in other words, the mind is the virtual body. The mind is a window through which people can look at the world and also themselves. Most often, the mind cognises the world, and ignores the process of recording. It is fulfilling to know what is in one's own backyard. The mind responds to the various stimuli it receives and functions in time. The situational awareness lets the mind decipher the world as it perceives. It recreates the past and also visualises the future. The nervous system carries signals from the body to the brain for processing. It maps a three-dimensional virtual world inside the brain.

The very feeling about the existence of the mind as distinct from the body calls for a deeper introspection of the nature of their relationship. Sometimes the body-mind complex tends to function as one entity. For instance, during extreme situations like a threat to life, there is total synchronisation between the body and the mind in a fight or flight choice. Whenever there is the body-mind fracture, it causes needless suffering and pain to the organism as a whole. The mind may want something knowing very well that the body is incapable of taking the strain. For example, the mind decides to do a marathon despite being aware of the condition of an arthritic knee. The body yields and the mind may temporarily win. In the long run, though, the whole organism breaks down due to this intransigence.

For the sake of convenience, one can label the content of the mind as the consciousness. There are several faculties and processes that help in maintaining and running of consciousness. They protect themselves from any debasement; they hold on to themselves as the conditioning dictates. The survival instinct acts for each and every cell and process within the organism.

Consciousness

Consciousness eludes a clear definition even with the present scientific scholarship. In this book, it means the entire content of the mind. This includes awareness, memory, ego, emotions, logic, conditioning *et cetera*. The entire virtual world is one's consciousness. Neurocognitive science offers theories, which posit the origin and workings of this extraordinarily important element in the human organism. Anaesthesia studies give a glimpse of the grades of consciousness one can experience. Psychedelic experimentations can also uncover the hidden recesses of consciousness. Brain-damaged subjects offer enormous clue to mapping different faculties to the spatial spread of the brain.

Realising the self-reflexive ability of the human brain is a free-for-all tool to look into one's own true nature. Attention to the ways of the mind opens up the door to consciousness. In this fascinating journey, all one requires is a bit of patience and commitment to unravel the hidden possibilities. One will reap enormous benefit in knowing and utilising the many processes that the species has sharpened over millions of years of evolution. Living beings are a combination of matter with respective shapes. The sum of the parts is certainly less than the whole. The difference is consciousness, but it does not exist without a physical body and vice versa. Consciousness is the toe-hold through which one can discover the self and the world.

Ego

Ownership or the ego is a map of all the nervous points of the body that feed into the brain. It is a unique identifier for the organism. This also creates separateness from others. There has always been the 'I' that is one's inner most sense of existence. It does not need another reference for its *raison d'être*. Every thought or activity connects invariably to the ego. The mind too forms an identity of its own. The ego also links this identity with the body. Body-mind identity is very deep rooted and gets formed in infancy itself.

The ego is necessary for all practical purposes. It enables the survival instinct and safeguards one from both external threats and auto-destruct tendencies. Ego also gives continuity to cognition. It is like a fulcrum on which everything gels. It produces a semblance of a false self within the head. If one were to map one's consciousness what will emerge, is a vast sense of blankness crowded with fleeting thoughts. Sometimes the ideas get meaningful and logical only when connected by the ego.

On the flip side, when the identification transcends the mind-body periphery, the ego tries to possess everything it surveys. Conflict in mind is not far off when the ego does not get its desires fulfilled. It manifests its vicious self-centeredness, overriding other important functions of the organism. The fallout of this is pain and suffering.

A whole book can be written on ego. Taming it when it either oversteps sanity or indulges itself in bloated fantasies is a sign of maturity. Ignorance of the self feeds on false identification. This vicious spiral has a movement of its own far removed from reality. To be centred is to be aware of entering the forests of imagination of one's own making. Only when clarity dawns on people that they realise where the purpose of ego ends and the wanderings of the mind begins.

Impulse

Any organism responds very fast when threatened suddenly. The instant response is via the reptilian brain activity. It bypasses the normal cognitive route and takes the required action immediately. Reptilian brain makes the body respond in times of emergency. The body has intelligence of its own that one cannot know consciously.

Awareness can see only part of the picture, which is probably the tip of the ice berg. There are many processes that run autonomously of which there is no self awareness. For example, conscious and subconscious levels of mind stand testimony to hidden decision-making. At the same time, one needs to appreciate that the data in the subconscious is nothing but knowledge one has gained in life. Impulsive behaviour is a result of such accumulation. It implies that one can be selective in retaining knowledge.

When individuals live in objectivity, they reject a subjective and irrational existence. One can even rewrite any old scripts of false beliefs and ideas in the light of discovery or knowledge. One need not be the rigid personalities of one's thinking. Witnessing these subtleties go a long way in self-discovery and transformation.

Memory

Memory is the data storehouse in the brain for the organism. Life will be impossible to be in *tabula rasa* always without this remarkable capacity. Memory, time and its perception have intrinsic links to one's future. Humans store not only names and numbers but also emotions, images, music, ideas, formulae and zillion other things. Medically speaking, when the brain gets worn out or diseased, memory fades. Old age too brings about forgetfulness. In scientifically terms, memory has short-term and long term characteristics. Scientists have not even scratched the surface on deciphering the mechanism of memory.

The human data warehouse works on associative properties. It retrieves meaning from the hidden folds of memory. To get a feel of it, visualise a thought experiment. *I try to recollect a face. I forget. I try hard. I get a face. I reject it as false. I try again. I get it.* This shows I have a reference to reject the false one even though I am unable to remember well the required one.

Right recognition is an interesting attribute of memory. The power of association, while storing things in memory is evident. Memory tags everything with a name, number, circumstance or something to be ready for recall. Storing any information needs a stamp of reference. Data has no meaning if there are no references for it. Even sound comes alive in reference to silence; only with differences does meaning arise. Unity cannot provide any definition or measure.

Humans hold on to conditioning stored in memory very tenaciously. They plod on even when they get bogged down by the weight of this baggage. Most often, the tyranny of bad events holds one hostage to suffering. Wallowing in sorrow over bad experiences is a particularly common human trait. Repeated and distressful memories clogging one's head triggers emotions and even sadness or depression. No one can erase one's own memory at will.

Whenever one encounters an emotional upheaval, it is a wake-up call to delve into oneself. Situational awareness helps one to accept only the essentials by ignoring all other data. Introspection makes people look into themselves objectively. In such exploration, one witnesses the mind functioning in clarity. It enables one to put everything in its place.

Mental inertia is very hard to break if one wrestles with it. In fact, it gets reinforced through more and more attention. Time could be a saver but is no panacea for deep-rooted attitudes. There is a lot of unproductive data in the back of everyone's mind. One can at least loosen the identification with all such burdens. The mental chatter loses its bite, eventually leaving witnessing pure as it always is. This is not escapism to forget worries temporarily.

Emotions

Emotions are natural and universal, which require no teaching. They humanise people and are the pillars of the mind. What one needs to learn, though, is how to mitigate the effects of uncontrolled emotional outbursts. Life without emotions will be dull and prosaic. One needs to embrace and experience all the emotions that occur within. Otherwise, one is poorer by the absence of the most life affirming gift of evolution. Emotions trigger bodily changes like spikes in hormones, blood pressure and temperature. It is a moot question if the physical changes come first, or the mental feelings produce them.

Essentially the organism wants to be peaceful. It responds to anything perceived to upset this state by a flurry of emotional signals. An action that is a consequence of such a virtual scream or wake-up call becomes an expression or behaviour. When people get emotional, they lose track of reality, flow with the rising tide and express themselves crudely. Depending on the situation, one may feel certain emotions rising within, creating the corresponding state of mind and action. In extreme situations, one may cry, shout or run to escape. Sometimes, the response could be to philosophise and blame it on fate. Ultimately, it is the survival technique of the organism to manufacture peace in the throes of mental outbursts.

What happens when one is in the thick of an emotional upheaval and lose all sanity and rationality? People make a mess of themselves and the world around them. Anger management has become a huge industry. Road rage is such a common phenomenon all over the world. Depression and other mental issues have more psychological origins than physiological reasons. Psychiatric drugs and counselling may give relief to extreme cases of emotional imbalance. Emotion being a situational response has energy of its own. Watching them without judgment brings tremendous peace irrespective of sadness or happiness rising within the mind. When sanity prevails, even when emotion rises in one's mind as a huge swell of energy, there is peace. In the same breath, one needs to understand that there can be no universal rule that can be applied to handle emotions. Each situation demands an original response.

Art will not be art if, not for emotions. In fact, classical Indian art characterises nine major emotions called the *navarasas*. The artists enact different emotions during performance. At the same time, they still retain their identity with their own centre of being. In other words, they do not get carried away by the passions they emote. One can use the same approach in one's life, as well.

Emotions need not be suppressed at all. One need not make detachment a hedge for sorrow. Understanding regret is different from being regretful. Similarly knowing anxieties are one thing, but wearing them while going about one's daily routine is another. To live well, one needs anger as much as love. It is legitimate to use anger when there is injustice. All the emotions are there for a cause, and it is frivolous to brand some as good and others bad. At the same time, the only caution is not to get trapped in emotions and lose one's ground.

Intelligence

Logic, rationality, common sense, ability, skill, brain power, grey matter and genius; these are some of the words, which mean the faculty of intelligence humans possess. The brain in its development has made a big leap in cognising, storing and manipulating known information. Every time it does not have to start from scratch. One builds on the wisdom from the past so that there is no need to reinvent the wheel. Art, science, commerce and all other human endeavours are consequences of the intellectual capabilities.

Intelligence makes one pick up new skills, research, organise and do many other things to progress in one's life. It is also about the way one adapts to changing situations. It could be done so by being cheerful and accepting things as they are. This can finally lead one to a fuller engagement with the universe. Intelligence cannot be limited to just IQ scores alone. The most striking aspect of intelligence translates into the techniques one develops to assimilate knowledge and reengineer that to one's individual and collective requirements.

Logic is clever. In every aspect of life one uses common sense. Current knowledge and situations in society dictate one to act appropriately. People rely on logic for survival. The skills that they pick up are directly helpful for them to survive in this world. Without rational ability, humans may be equivalent to animals in the wild. Rationality has a major part to play in survival and comfortable living. It has directly ushered in material progress and more knowledge among people.

Eating, mating and defending may be common to all species on earth. Humans are a cut above the rest because of their pattern-matching capability and to work towards a goal based on their knowledge and experience. All faculties interrelate with each other and as such, cannot be viewed in isolation. For the sake of convenience, intelligence is highlighted here. People could engage themselves for the common good of society and inch forward in realising their potential and purpose. On the contrary, if people dawdle or still worse, feed on the system for evil and partisan agenda, the entire society takes a beating in progress and evolution.

There are of course certain dimensions in life where intelligence fails. Relying on it totally as a panacea for all ills will not bear any dividends. The fundamental questions of existence, for instance, cannot be answered by logic. Being or the sheer beauty of existence has no logic to it. In a lighter vein, when one is with one's partner, more than reason, passion carries weight. On the contrary, in office, it will be disastrous to use emotions when solid reasoning needs to be the foundation. Similarly, even though musical structures have logic behind them, one needn't get punctilious to appreciate a moving piece. Enjoy the emotions in music as much as one is in awe when digesting a path-breaking judicial judgment.

Responsibility, sense and sensibility are all attributes of intelligence. One must embrace intelligence in action. Additionally, acknowledge the strengths and limitations of each and every faculty one possesses. The individuals' awareness and conscious thinking aid them towards realising these simple processes.

Will

Will is about becoming. Desires take shape into goal and goads people into action. Survival instinct makes people achieve their goals through the power of will. When actions bear fruits, one is proud of the will power and its benefits. It is strange that many people never get content with desiring what they can have. This is not to suggest that aspirations and goals are redundant. Motivation kicks in and gives one the ability to satisfy one's desires. Focus and self-confidence are qualities that are necessary to translate any burning desire to accomplish things through the power of will.

Many successful people have worked against all odds, to get what they wanted in life. Trial and achievement need not always go hand in hand. People pacify themselves; after all, they are destiny's children. Especially in failures one would have thought of the power of will and destiny playing in one's life. Those ideas are the mental cushion to support one who falters.

There is a tendency of the mind to link a cause and effect in everything it surveys. In responding objectively to any situation, there is totality of action. Similarly, objectivity needs to be inculcated when witnessing the workings of one's mind, as well. Then there will not be suffering from the ideas of either will or destiny. When one has the will to overcome destiny and let destiny have that will, there is effortless action. Being aware of the task in hand and using the power of will intelligently is right action.

Realisation is not a state achieved over a period through will power. It does not belong to the future either. The question of when one can realise, implies time, future, hope or effort. Ideas of what one should be; suppress the effortless, joyous and ever-present nature of existence. One is in it right now; in a way, one is that. Anything that triggers this transcendence to happen is indeed the need of the hour.

Thought

The basic transactional currencies, for the virtual body, are the firing of neurons. This constant play of millions of electrochemical activities involves neuro-transmitters in the brain. It makes beings cognise the world, have emotions, sharpen intelligence and above all think. All the organs and faculties thrive on interdependence. There is logic in emotions. There are emotions in powering the logic, as well. Factually, nothing of these can be separated to make them into independent entities.

Awareness makes one conscious of whatever runs in the brain. Being awake to the thoughts is a result of that action. Attention aids one to focus on desired things. All the exchanges that occur within the brain are out of bound of consciousness. The manifestations of some of these processes come to the surface of consciousness, and one can perceive them. There is a long way to go before one can be more definitive on brain science.

Is it possible to think of two things at the same time?

At any given moment, there can be only one representation of the state of the brain. The brain waves correspond to the state of the neural network. There cannot be another neural signature beside the one manifested in the brain. There may be continuous streams of ideas that the brain whips up. One cannot assume that there are multiple states of the brain at the same time. Awareness reads even the ego or the sense of self as a passing thought. There is no permanent resident 'I' sitting inside one's head. Ego is an illusion, but it gives continuity and a sense of connection to the clouds of fleeting thoughts and feelings in the brain. One feels, 'all these happen to me'.

Rest thought

Activities occupy everyone from birth until death. The demands, in this action-packed world, are numerous; one needs to run faster to stay put in one place. As a consequence, there is frustration. Stress level goes up, and listening goes down. There is a need to rejuvenate one's health to continue with activities. For instance, an intellectual labourer may treat taking rest as physical inactivity. On the other hand, an intellectual labourer may opt for a gym work-out to chill. In order to break the monotony of activities, people need diversions for both the body and mind.

There are many organs in the body that cannot rest. The heart for instance does not stop even for a minute in one's entire life. The blood flow, breath and so many other involuntary bodily activities go on unhindered till death. The organism cannot freeze even for a moment; it at least builds stories in its mind. One may desperately yearn for a rest, just to escape from the humdrum of life. Unfortunately, even vacations and entertainment fail to bring any permanent cheer. Rest is a myth; what one talks about is only diversion.

Is there a way out of this madness?

The world is a reflection of one's thoughts. Everyone is in a runaway mode, in today's rat race. There is hardly a serene moment in one's existence where one is free from the perennial demands of either mental or physical activity. People who are inactive may appear physically calm. Appearances are deceptive; they may still be furiously acting mentally. In fact, for many who are in stress, even sleep is an activity and dreams burden it further.

One cannot be productive when one is tired. Nevertheless, the mind can make even a knackered body run to satisfy its whims. Thought builds some momentum of its own. The body becomes a slave. The pressure of thought on the organism is very much under rated. It breaks the delicate synchronism of the body-mind complex. Thought has a voracious appetite. It builds emotions, spawns more thoughts and looks out for patterns in the world endlessly. No wonder, rest is so difficult to come by for people pursuing it.

Nobody can live if they banish thoughts from their system. The real rest happens when one gives rest to thought. That can happen when thought ceases to be the driver. Only then, the organism functions freely without stress. When thought is in its place, it becomes a tool. It functions when necessary, or thought processes remain a silent potential and be ready to act.

In witnessing, there is effortlessness and optimum functioning of all the processes in the organism. There is no fatigue or stress in the seamless integration of thinking and action. Even when there is a continuous activity, there will be an experience of complete rest. Rest is not cessation of activities. Even for a moment one can never take rest. On the contrary, it is clarity and knowledge that bring effortlessness in one's life.

Self Awareness

All living beings possess awareness in varying degrees of manifestation. The seat of awareness for humans is the nervous system and the brain. Self-awareness is a unique faculty humans possess. Only humans have evolved to a great degree in experiencing self-reflection, situational awareness and contemplation. Modern theories suggest mirror neurons responsible for this Lamarckian evolutionary leap.

There are two divergent schools of thoughts to the origin of awareness; materialism and spiritualism. The materialists explain it away as an epiphenomenon; a consequence of matter in the right arrangement. For the materialists, the sum of the parts equals the whole. The spiritualists, on the other hand, claim it is akin to the *élan vital* and pinnacle of life itself. It stands out of the field of matter in which everything else belongs to in living beings. There has been a tendency, especially by the spiritualists to treat awareness as the key to all knowledge. For some of them, the brain is an instrument which acts like an antenna that captures thoughts from the universe.

The thought-sphere is the Big Mind which holds all the information of the past, present and future.

Is awareness a dimension within that one can fathom and from whence existence and its concomitant questions get answered?

Doubtless without awareness, humans would not be what they are today. At the same time, one need to accept that awareness as a faculty has its limitation. It cannot know the processes happening deep within one's own body, let alone have answers to critical issues of existence. The workings of enzymes or the organs are in the dark. One can cognise just what registers in the consciousness. Only with the progress of neurocognitive sciences one may envisage defining the basis of awareness.

There is no question of taking positions in the war between materialists and spiritualists. As matters stand today, it will be silly in claiming one school of thought as superior to the other. It is fascinating to utilise the given faculties to the fullest extent by realising oneself better.

To explain the sense of perception, a crude comparison will be like putting things on the table of awareness. Awareness is the ability to make consciousness register all thoughts and sensations as they are happening. Without it, one would not even know one's own existence. One can act in a given situation blindly or with awareness. A simple example could be the difference between hearing and listening. In listening objectively, there is empathy, in addition to the recording of, mere sounds as in hearing.

Awareness gives life to both the conscious mind and its counterpart, the subconscious mind. Whatever sublimates from the hidden realms of the self gets noticed due to the action of awareness. The role of awareness in cognising the visible opportunity of daily life is a taken. Sensations and cerebral processes bring to life the world and ideas.

Awareness enables the formation of individual identities. It helps one to watch emotions wax and wane and utilises intelligence to navigate through the maze of living. When it comes to memory, it lets one travel in a virtual time machine that recalls data stored in the brain. On a lighter note, awareness makes one talk about oneself critically and humorously to live life as it is.

Engaging with situations in complete awareness is adapting to situations. It is quite habitual to go on an auto-pilot in one's actions. When there is lack of attention with the inner or outer world, one gets lost. This is the genesis of boredom and also the constant urge to satiate the thirst for more and more sensations. People turn restive because they want variety in their lives. When one adapts, the emphasis is no more on sensations per se but on the spirit of engaging with life itself.

Life presents individuals with so many things every moment. Ego comes in the way of adaptation as much as the fear of losing one's conditioning. All these impediments hold people back from embracing change. Adaptation allows one to be conscious of the need to embrace fully one's body, mind and society. Then there is more clarity, purpose and awareness in life.

Language

Language is the link between the organism and the outside world. It is the mysterious link humans have with their own selves as they talk incessantly to themselves, as well. Language is a universal human trait. Humans have developed thousands of languages, many connected to each other in vocabulary or grammar. It is one of the greatest mile stones in evolution.

It goes without saying that language is one of the fundamental aspects of humanness. Apart from being a tool for laying bare thoughts for communication, language finds expression in venting emotions as poetry or lyrics, framing precise equations for science and chants or prayers for supposedly getting connected with the divine.

What breath is to the body, so is language to the mind. It is impossible to think of a life without acquiring language skills. Language is a medium to transmit information and culture. This glue has held societies together throughout civilisation. The world one creates in one's head gets conveyed through this magic. Otherwise, people will inhabit in their own worlds disconnected with the rest of society. However imperfect language might be to express one's mind precisely; one cannot dispense with it to live in this world.

Language is basic to life. It has the power to, condition, as well as, make one understand one's conditioning. Realisation is neither an object nor an idea that fits a description. One may wonder as to the role of language in one's seeking. Seeking and the veracity of language, indeed have a tenuous bond. There may be possibilities for misinterpretation, even with 'precise' language. People with vested interests interpret many religious texts written thousands of years ago into terror manuals. The world struggles today for answers.

Is the language the culprit for the misunderstanding of scriptures? Could the blame, be rather, one's mental incapability to decipher the same? Whatever it is, humanity is walking on the thin edge of a knife. One's interpretation depends on conditioning and what one wants to make out of a text. Metaphors and symbolism in texts make matters worse. Moreover, language being dynamic, it changes form and meaning from time to time. Realisation cannot be trapped in the narrow confines of language. It is, therefore, very important to know how and where to use proper language to disseminate ideas coherently.

Meaning

In the process of finding meaning to a sentence, the mind scans through the concept of each word or phrase that one already knows. As one reads, the mind takes one to the concept of each word or phrase that one stores in memory. For instance, take the sentence, "The cat chases a rat." One might have perhaps imagined a cat that is chasing a rat. The images may be distinct for different people at different times. It is fascinating that as one reads, word by word, one is creating an incremental mental imagery that evolves into the overall meaning of the sentence.

Thus, the overall meaning emerges out of the connection of the individual bits and pieces of information. One may then act upon that information as one's intuitions suggest. For instance, if the information is somehow important, one may commit it to memory. One then goes to the next sentence, and the process continues.

This deluge of information gets selectively stored in the brain. Language experience and also the signals from the five senses are the data inputs. The interpretations from them reinforce one's memory. Some concepts get strengthened, and others weakened in one's mind. From the *tabula rasa* in one's childhood, language faculty is shaped to the present state of development. In fact, this conditioning enables one to derive meaning from a string of words in the first place. The continuous feedback loop involving the inputs and conditioning mould one's relationship with the world.

Common language

The most vital element for communication is language. In ancient times, as of now, people who spoke different languages depended on translators. People used to live in small groups or tribes and might not have travelled like the modern humans. Wars and conquests were common, and the victor normally imposed their language and culture on the vanquished. The language in courts was that of the conquerors. The vast majority of the ordinary people continued with their own tongue.

Things took a different turn with the advent of the British ruling the seas. They conquered many lands in all the continents. The Sun never set in the British Empire. The British naturally planted English in almost all corners of the world. America is another major power that speaks English and is a champion of trade and commerce. In the last decade, the internet too contributed enormously in spreading English all through the world.

There are far-reaching consequences to this evolving phenomenon. Language is not neutral and comes with ideas and thought processes of its native speakers. It is a package that rubs off the culture of its origin, subtly on the speaker. In this scenario will it be preposterous to consider that other tongues may become extinct in the course of time? Will English, in one form or the other then, become the language of the future; the *lingua franca* of the whole world? This development may be heralding the globalisation of humanity through a common language.

Some non native English speakers feel subjugated in having to speak an alien language in their daily lives. Others do it to get better reach and audience for their trade and services. The native speakers at least some of them, feel superior and try to control others through the power of their mother tongue. English seems to be eclipsing other languages. There are many such unintended consequences that have come about with this trend.

From an unbiased attitude, one can see the opportunity to look at language as another tool to express oneself. Ideally, people should not identify with the language they like. One has to realise the quirks of history, and neither curse nor gloat over them. Then, one stands a better chance in knowing one's true identity. The same logic applies to religion, nationality, culture and race, as well. There are many such things one tenaciously holds on to, forgetting the very essence of the spirit of commonality all people have. All these variables are expressions for the organism to interact and enliven itself as part of its existence here. One can truly embrace each other with outward differences in a spirit of camaraderie. It can happen, if only there is no prejudice against persons professing divergent views and behaviour.

The Impressions

Knowledge is power. Does it mean that all the available knowledge is real? When one is unable to decide the veracity of what one holds deep within the mind, there could be a conflict. There may be even times when one's experiences corroborate with one's beliefs. The devil is in the temptation, and it is natural to fall for it. When wisdom dawns, is one ready to adapt to the new knowledge or tie oneself up in knots with the old, yet cherished tinsel? Awareness of the impressions will help break the dead-weight of knowledge one accumulates.

Knowledge, experience and conditioning, are the impressions that give shape to the personality which one carries for one's entire life. Impressions from many sources bombard one throughout life. Some of them go to the core of one's being and get stored for life while others fade in memory, as trivial. The patterns that one select could be from the earliest impressions in childhood. Being aware of these subtle forces brings in more clarity. It then becomes easier, to resolve pain and complexes in one's consciousness.

Knowledge comes from several quarters, and experiences accumulate moment to moment. As age goes by, these make one's sack of conditioning bulkier and rigid. To give an example, statistics show that the world population stands at seven billion and still counting. It is doubtful that this knowledge has percolated down to the masses. On the contrary, human reproductive behaviour reflects the attitude differently. Environmental damage is another reckless action that calls for urgent repair. The knowledge is out there, but old habits die hard.

There is a mismatch between one's conditioning and knowledge of the times. People fall asunder by the inevitable pushes and pulls of their own making. Veritable knowledge of reality needs to trickle down to one's bones. There are many impressions one unwittingly carries on one's back. In total attention, one can break the impasse and adapt to any challenge.

A question may crop up as to what it means to be in total attention. The world appears to people based on their background. What is good for the goose need not be good for the gander. Understanding and responding to situations depend on one's impressions. The adjectives one has of any experience get carried over to any new situation one encounters in the future, as well. The impressions project the same response repeatedly like a script in one's mind. This unconscious behaviour may block one from taking right actions in one's life. The scripts can be likened to clouds covering a mountain, and attention to that of the Sun. When one is in complete attention, the scripts evaporate making the mountain of knowledge clearly visible for one to see. Decision making and consequent action will then be a breeze.

One needs to bridge the gap between knowledge, experience and conditioning. One may act objectively on the impressions gained in life to turn oneself from a controlled passive robot to a liberated active human being. One is then able to live in clarity, abandoning the scripts of confounding conditioning.

Knowledge

Sense perceptions limit one's knowledge intake. Apart from these inputs, one has no other means, from any other source, to unravel the mystery of existence. Humans have been exploring, everything in the universe, right from the dawn of civilisation. It is natural for a stranded person in an island to explore the place. The same has been happening with humanity in a larger context. As a collective legacy, the earlier generations have been passing on their wisdom to their offspring.

Knowledge is more than mere data. It is the ability of an organism to cognise, process as well as to communicate information with oneself and others. The brain is the centre of consciousness where all knowledge transactions run. Acquiring knowledge about something is to understand the workings of the object in question. It is a chain of many things and faculties working in tandem. The various forms of knowledge like law, art, medicine and science, help people look at reality from different perspectives.

Humans have been doggedly scanning the vastness of space, as well as, straining to peep into the smallness of atoms. This pursuit to understand the habitat rewards great bounties. Scientists may be able to decipher many secrets of nature, in the times to come. They aim to shrink the space of the unknown to zero in their attempts to demystify the universe. The quest for total knowledge is of course a collective endeavour and cannot be an individual accomplishment alone.

Knowledge conveys meaning upon meaning on everything one surveys. One thinks and ferrets out information to a remarkable degree of astonishment about many things in nature. There is still knowledge pouring in from various labs around the world. It is work in progress, and all these efforts have helped to understand the world better.

The true spirit of enquiry is not to let any stone unturned, for scientific answers. Fortunately, in many institutions and countries, this temper holds sway. There may be *cul-de-sacs* on the way. Whenever, there is a deeper insight into the way nature works, it is cause for jubilation. The quest for wisdom should draw more laurels and encouragement from society.

Ocean of knowledge; not a drop of peace

People dream of perennial joy while living and bliss after death. The knowledge of peace and immortality is a deeply ingrained idea in many people around the world. Knowledge has provided tremendous impetus for people to learn more about nature. In every country, there is a consensus, if not action, for development and progress for its citizens. In fact, the world has come out of the dark ages in terms of comfort and convenience for many of its people. However, one knows from experience that knowledge is no guarantee to peace.

Even a cursory glance reveals that starvation, unsustainable population, suffering and brutality are rampant in this world. The common man is unable to lead a happy and prosperous life. One cannot say if the individual is to be corrected or the collective to be blamed for this transgression. No one can ignore the soft underbelly of society, which holds the hunger of billions of deprived lives.

Peace and stability, equitable distribution of planetary resources, and evolution encompassing the known are visibly absent in all societies. Fissures due to political, national and religious divisions are increasing by the day. Even on an individual level humans are a lost lot. Peace despite assimilating knowledge seems to be utopian. There is an inadequacy in one's approach to correct collective failures. The hard-earned knowledge of the centuries does not seem to help people at large. It has not diminished anxieties and insecurities of the future. The long shadow of dark ages still looms over societies. They fight with airplanes and missiles now, instead of, chariots and arrows of the past centuries.

Unfortunately, people do not live in the totality of knowledge; rather than the norm, it is the exception. People fail to embrace their experience and knowledge fully. If they do attempt, it could enrich their incomplete lives into a harmony. Many limit their *umwelt* to fulfil their creature-comforts alone. After all, people want to satisfy what their conditioning dictates. For them, life is neither an expression nor a responsibility to integrate one's impressions. As a consequence, a fracture emerges in the awareness of one's impressions. Engaging the world from fullness will alone be the hallmark of wisdom.

The main drag to change is the enormous weight of conditioning. Everyone harbours, un-corrected and often, unrecognised knowledge as true. It rears its ugly head as superstitions, addictions, false imaginings, fears, unsocial behaviour and the like. One holds on to the same patterns of habits and tradition in one's upbringing. It effectively prevents the percolation of genuine wisdom into the bag of scripts one carries in memory. The insouciance towards integrating the impressions of life will be at one's own peril.

The myth of omniscience

Awareness is a local phenomenon within the body. It processes whatever corporal signals that come its way. In fact, it cannot cognise data which the body cannot access. It is futile to imagine the organism holding a pervasive universal sense of awareness. The scope of the human organism is not for that at all. Even the unconscious processes happening within the body are beyond the scope of its grasp. To claim that one has evolved to take in all the knowledge of the universe or being omniscient is mere megalomania.

Humans perceive through the sense organs and have the ability to process stored information. One then creates a map of cognition in one's consciousness. There is a division of labour in gathering signals for cognition and also a time lapse in processing them. Instantaneous knowledge is another myth people have perpetuated. It is certainly second hand information one takes in the brain.

Is total knowledge only a dream? The rational mind uses logic to go to the source of all things experienced and imagined by it. The mystical mind, on the other hand, has faith in the unknown for illumination. If an entity claims total knowledge, it implies three hundred and sixty degree attention at all times. The entity must also be able to communicate the registered information to itself or to the outside world. This is absurd and beyond the capability of a human being. The idea of total knowledge is only the fancy of the human mind.

One also has to contextualise knowledge and behaviour of individuals. It is essential to consider the times of their lives, in doing so. Prior to the advancement of science, hygiene would have been just an idea of cleanliness. Suppose someone had physical proximity with a patient suffering from an infectious disease. The prevalent customs or a sense of good will might have made him act that way. Even a saint might have been unhygienic, by today's standards. Fast-forward to the twentieth century; there is knowledge that avoiding infection requires disinfectants. A person in peace may be carrying on with good intention. Such a deed may turn out wrong if there is lack of knowledge. Proper integration of knowledge with behaviour is necessary for harmony in society.

Thus, even behaviour cannot be an attribute for realisation if not embraced in the spirit of knowledge. In fact, realisation cannot be defined at all by any tell-tale marks. Strangely, society always tends to defend realised people as infallible and ever virtuous. Fundamentalism and literal interpretation of old scriptures fall under this category. To this day, the vast majority of people are slaves to the thought processes of even ancient prophets and seers. As a result of conflicting competitiveness among the different followers, there are bigotry and divisions in the world. One simply refuses to move with the times.

Realisation is not a fantasy of evolving into a *übermensch* capable of total knowledge. It is not in identifying with the unknown, either. People suppose that omniscience is one of the attributes of the unknown. Unfortunately, billions of people swear by the words of such claimants. Theocracies even run nations on these principles. Realising one's own capabilities and possibilities opens up more freedom, and less stress in acquiring such impossible feats. It also saves one from the deceptions by those leaders.

Experience

The bodily features of Homo sapiens have not changed much, since their evolution. One experiences different sensations, thanks to the sense organs. The body enables movement in space and communication through language. In addition to the physical experiences, one also creates an inner world that gives the sense of time along with space. There is pain which one avoids and pleasure or satisfaction one desires. One grows from the stage of an infant to an adult. A couple reproduces and nurtures young ones. In old age, everyone returns to a second childhood and eventually dies. This is essentially the human experience.

Experience of oneself and the world ripens with the knowledge about them. Losing memory will seal the fate of all experiences, as well. Experiences are sensory and also cerebral in nature. People crave for certain experiences over and over again because they like them. Illusion of validity is the false belief that one accepts as true. For example, everyone sees the Sun always rising in the east. It is true, but a furtherance of knowledge has taught that it is indeed the earth's revolution around the Sun which causes the said experience. Experience alone is not enough to represent any situation. Knowledge too is necessary to complete the story.

Conditioning

Assume the human organism as a black box. At any given point of time, one is a bundle of living cells and organs giving shape to one's body. The current stimuli and conditioning determine a person's response to any situation in life. Inputs of matter, energy and data return an output in a different form. Nature and nurture work together. People constantly interact with the environment and respond accordingly. One has no control over the input that happens in the present. Therefore, the only variable is the conditioning one carries all the time. A proper understanding of that has a great bearing on the future.

Consciousness carries the memory of knowledge and experiences. These are directly or indirectly influenced by conditioning. The tools for survival are conditioning along with one's body. So conditioning is the nerve-centre of one's knowledge and experience.

Humans do not exist to experience the moment alone. The wisdom of ancestors has gone deep into the collective consciousness. It has created the conditioning on how to organise society as a group and to live dutifully. One carries the conditioning of thousands of generations. It is especially intriguing to see how the so-called realised men have influenced human thought and conditioning. That is also part of one's story. The conditioning continues with the new stories one makes.

Conditioning is neither good nor bad. It is neutral, just like the knowledge or experience illumining the consciousness. Millions of years of evolution have made a dent in the brain. It is easily able to hold all the relevant information the organism gathers. One adapts to a position based on past knowledge. The key to successful living is not in effacing conditioning. On the contrary, one needs to be aware of even the subtle workings of the same. Then there is integration of the impressions, namely, knowledge, experience and conditioning.

∞: THE ORGANISATION OF THE SELF AND SOCIETY

Are the organisation of the self and society, the same? Individual interests vary widely from that of society's necessities. Survival of both is a given, though. There are infinite connections between the two. In the same breath, there are differences too, in reaching consensus among individuals on many social issues. Evolution on a collective basis shifts the focus among individuals from self-interest and competition to sensitivity and interdependence. This evolution in mass consciousness is the pressing need of the times. It begins with each and every one, and when one lives in freedom; it can lead to genuine progress in the world.

The Self

The individual is what the individual does. Black or white, rich or poor, tall or short, believer or non-believer, man or woman; one can abstract the commonalities of the individual's function. A single person is not a lone entity but live in relation to other people, ideas, things, animals, plants and everything else in the universe.

One may think, "Where is the kick in relationships if one cannot possess them". Individuals need to control and claim everything in the entire universe. Infinite desires would want unlimited possessions. The party cannot go on merrily as individuals fail to get, results and answers, for all their wants. There is also angst, which is nothing but a thorn in the flesh, which breaks their ego to smithereens.

The individual is not supreme. One feels that there is something more to be subdued, and until then life is unfulfilled. This is the human predicament which brings in laughter, tears, superiority and at times helplessness. Irrespective of the emotions, there is a joy in one's presence on the planet and mystery in leaving invisible foot-prints in the universe.

Individuals make up community. Therefore, it is important to realise how they organise themselves individually and also collectively. There are commonalities as well as differences among individuals in a society. There are four major areas one acts upon in life. Firstly, health is vital for purposeful living. Then the need arises for people to relate with the world, in general, and people in particular. The mind does not go to sleep with this alone. It now wants to control or possess what it surveys. Finally, if the *objet d'desire* does not come through, the individual panics and gets anxious.

All activities are invariably to satisfy both the body and mind. Healthy living is maintaining the organism ship-shape. Relationships nurture interdependence, among people and things, in the world. Ultimately, it matures in relating with the universe itself. The mind covets things and ideas that it desires. Possessions in life are not only for existence, but also for extravagance. Desires could range from material to Meta physical things. Last but not the least, there is always the wonder of the universe and the perennial existential angst.

For a comfortable living, many people need to struggle endlessly. The result is a mixed bag of success and failures. If only one is objective, existence is beautiful in this planet. The individual is never alone in this world. One relates to something or someone always. Success lies in being aware of the interdependence of everything in the world.

Health

Mens Sana in Corpore Sano is the basis for one's well being. Until death, one needs a healthy body and mind to function well in life. Absence of diseases alone cannot be a measure of wellness. Health has its foundation in both nature and nurture. There cannot be any control over the genes one inherits, but one can always live responsibly. Well being, is the clichéd unity of, '*manasa, vacha, karmana*', in one's life.

The organism is one, even though it has many parts, which may seem to be acting independently. In realising this, there is no more fragmentation, isolation or indulgence by the individual. The body and mind arise in the same organism. Realising the criticality of their influence on each other, one can effortlessly usher in a healthy life. Then one can experience harmony between the body, mind, and even the larger environment.

There are overarching factors in people's minds regarding the concept of health and survival. The perception of a right body is one such hard-to-knock-off fact. People go for any length to attain the elixir of life. Even cosmetic surgeries and diet-starvation have become common fads among the youth. Fantasising about a perfect body or mind is unhealthy and detrimental to health.

The world looks at sensations, more for their entertainment value than functional utility. Sensual experiencing is beautiful, provided one connects it to the organism. Bereft of this totality in mind, it becomes skewed and one sided. People yield to sense gratifications, as well, that are available so freely at the cost to their health.

An instance is the abuse of ears by listening to songs at very high volume using headphones. The delicate ear-drum may even get ruptured. One may enjoy the sound temporarily at the expense of a hearing loss. Opting for a sensation driven existence, seems to be catching up in the consumerist world of today. One must rather, examine one's indulgences objectively, for a stress-free life.

Survival is the basis for life, ingrained in every organism. Surprisingly, one goes against this true tenet of life. There is a dichotomy between survival instinct and indulgence. When the latter overrides the former, there is disarray. The villain is the identification one develops in the mind. The complete attention on the mind will foster the right action.

Addiction is a function of wanting to experience the same sensations repeatedly. Many people have vices ranging from drugs to tobacco. There is also the indulgence in junk food. These habits make one suffer lifelong debilitating conditions. Finally, one may need medication to get better. Knowledge alone has not encouraged people to do the right things all the time.

Conditioning overturns sanity, and pulls the mind and body through a vicious spiral of insensitive attitude and behaviour. It rules all decision making when there is a lack of attention. Consequently, there is division between the body and mind. One slips from reality and identifies with what one harbours in mind.

There is *joie de vivre* when the whole organism with its multi-faculties of the mind and bodily processes, work in tandem. There is an effortless approach towards health, when they integrate with the organism as a whole. Only then one will not indulge in satisfying sensations at the cost of one's health. Fitness succeeds in total attention to the diverse pulls of the body and mind.

The human body is subject to natural transition from infancy to old age. The body goes through the growth phase initially, and then it decays. People perceive youth and the associated development as good, whereas, aging and death cause fear about their irreversibility. Confronting entropy, as if it were an enemy is not clarity. There is always the inevitability of change. This understanding helps one lead a life style appropriate to one's age and condition. Tending to old or ill people is also a test of one's resolve in accepting these human conditions.

Food as medicine and medicine as food, along with proper exercise, are important to healthy living. Both action and leisure are essential to keep body and mind well. In short, the body-mind conundrum need not be left as an eternal conflict.

Self-discovery starts with one's body and mind. It acts as a gateway to know oneself and also the environment one belongs to always. The subject of study, the object of observation, as well as, the tool for doing these are all rolled into one's own organism. Being aware of the impressions one carries, helps one to live healthy. It benefits individuals, society and also the larger environment everyone is part of.

Relationship

A healthy existence and purposeful relationships go hand in hand. One relates not only to other people, but also to oneself, things and ideas. Relationships play a major role in being a mirror to know each other, as well as, the whole world. A simple thought experiment can demonstrate the power of relationship. "Take away everyone from one's life. Is life possible then?" In fact, survival depends on relationships.

Humanity is a web of relationships in the present, which are spun from the past and cast into the future. Love and myriad other emotions well up in any human interaction. Tackling them take up a major chunk of one's life. Separation or death can snatch away near and dear ones. Broken relationships are the cause for broken hearts. People look for security through relationships. They act as filling up the dots in one's life.

Finding meaning to one's linkages is the basis of any relationship. The birth of any child delivers the birth of many relationships. The genetic codes shape biological forms. One imbibes culture and tradition from one's parents and fore fathers. The body and mind have ancestry. Everyone has an inherent relationship with everyone else physiologically and also psychologically. It makes sense due to the shared genes and culture. Nobody is an orphan.

One looks for a link or connection with another for bonding. It could be physical, intellectual or emotional in nature, and fosters responsibility in one's mind on the other. Normally, it happens with the identification people have for religion, nationality or family. They feel togetherness in such networks. When people relate to strangers, new ideas or even places, they may have to overcome mental blocks before establishing intimacy. Acceptance comes only with openness and empathy.

The images one creates about oneself, and others are only conditional. When one relates to others based on such a false pretence, there may be more divisions and misunderstanding. Watchfulness provides the understanding of one's own true nature. In total attention to the ways of one's mind, one will neither expect from nor yield to another in a dysfunctional relationship. It is not to be mistaken as selfishness at all. On the contrary, there is love without any adulteration of bondage in living with one and all. Then relating with others becomes easy and fruitful.

Chasing a goal of making bonds of steel with everyone else in the planet will not bring a revolution in building relationships. In fact, anything forced from outside will not stand the test of time. The world has tried this with many, ifs and buts, through ideology, religion and coercion. These have only fuelled the constriction of people's minds. Complete attention to one's own self is the sure-fire-way to let relationships bloom.

Relationships define any person's life, howsoever famous or ordinary; one might be. There are constraints in defining and nurturing one's ties with people. The glue of duty, attachment and love, limits people to have only a few relatives and friends. Except perhaps for these cherished things and people, one is unable to be genuinely close with all in society.

One can vouch from experience that, especially, failures in relationships play a major role in triggering the quest for knowing one's place in the world. People are most often toxic in their behaviour, and cause both physical and mental problems to each other. In extreme cases, they get depressed, murder or commit suicide when they fail in relationships. This happens when their expectations are not met from the others they value. Relationship is made out to be a function of the other. In reality, one makes or mars relationship based on one's own mind.

Knowing any relationship has to begin with understanding oneself. How is one connected to the body, mind, elements, senses, breath and many other processes one is endowed with, in life? Self-discovery uncovers the relationship with one's self, as well as, others. In a cosmic level, it brings home the awareness of one's relatedness with the universe itself. The true relationship flowers only when one discovers one's own nature.

Self-discovery initiates people to observe everything happening around them from objectivity. When relationship is an idea, there could be expectations and betrayal. If there is total engagement based on objectivity, there is joy. There are emotions and logic in human linkages. Love is usually a prisoner in relationships. It is because traditions define them. Self-discovery lets love free.

Possession

Human nature is to posses or at least control, what it wants to relate. The mind wants to be in the spot light always. It feels superior when it perceives to be in command. Possessions bring the mind security and an ego boost. One forgets that the mind is a tool that can be used for certain things. It is excellent in its design and purpose. The sloppy mind oversteps its brief and wants ownership of everything it desires.

The mind wants to possess things, people, ideas and even immortality, if possible. It fails repeatedly and rarely learns the hard lesson in knowing the right thing it needs. Once the mind knows its place, life becomes delightful. Until then, desires multiply with ferocity and ignore the assets of the individual. This waywardness leaves people with only sorrow and bitterness of not being in control.

Material advancement has provided humankind with a deluge of attractive range of goods and services. Society has created momentum of its own to tempt people to possess these. They believe that everything advertised, is for them to consume. Then they struggle with hope, to digest the drudgery of these desires.

Possess what one can use and do not bite what one cannot chew. If things are for instantaneous use like food in a buffet, one is content with what one needs at the moment. Ego and uniqueness could also drive people wanting to own something special. For instance, a stone from the moon which Neil Armstrong brought to earth will be a prized possession.

Money can convert most of the desires anytime, and that fuels greed. Imagine a waste-disposal company offers all the neighbourhood garbage to local residents. By all probabilities, they may not accept it. In case, the company offers cash in lieu of the garbage everyone may take it. The basic currency of goods and services is clean, ever acceptable and never a burden to possess.

This is not an ideal world with a secure future. Cataclysmic changes to the world could topple one's living standards. One takes for granted the bare necessities available in life. People are ever after luxury in their lives. Technology offers a partial solution. The mantra is to possess or perish. People want to possess money and what it can buy. The list does not stop there, and includes people, power, children and privileges, as well.

The whole world believes that progress is complementary to possession. The effects are; more mountains turned into buildings, forests denuded, and rivers emptied, all to satisfy the insatiable covetousness of people. Populations increase by the billions since everyone wants to possess children. The stress to possess scarce resources fuels fierce competition among nations, states and individuals. As a whole, the quality of living of the peoples around the world is dismal. Where does one go from here?

It is clearly unsustainable if people want to have personal cars and planes. If everyone thinks of having many children or has multiple unused apartments, it is a case of greed. These are unimaginative ways to boost one's self worth. Genuine need is everything and image is nothing. The world is at a crossroads now. It is time to decide if one wants to be rational or go down the road to perdition.

The spirit of genuine enquiry needs to be always welcome. It will let people make conscious choices in all interactions. One needs to possess only to survive with dignity in this world. This simple shift in one's approach to life will go a long way in sharing valuable resources and ideas with all of humanity. The world can certainly be a better place.

Angst

When desires turn unreal, there is anxiety. Somehow one wants to own one's desires at any cost. Many times, the results and one's expectations do not match. Nevertheless, one picks up new threads again to spin more cloth. Material living is an endless play of expectation, action and result. In some instances, one may get results of one's liking. It is natural to believe that one can achieve any wish fulfilled with the right combination of action. Problems multiply when one desires answers for the fundamental questions of life. Searching them through science is one thing; fantasising on delusions of others, turns people into zombies.

Can angst ever go away from one's mind?

Angst exists in everyone who wants to know life and death, space and time and everything between matter and spirit. It lies dormant and wakes up only to remind the insignificance and ignorance of the existence. It irritates the ego which then devises a fantastic after-life and heaven, as solutions. There are issues because one lives. Birth, life, death and all their concomitant problems have spurred people to rationalise their existence. Knowledge has unravelled the many mysteries of the universe. The fundamental questions though, still play truant.

The human organism is functional with various faculties. It knows its capabilities and limitations of deciphering reality. The mind imagines and builds up stories to quench its existential curiosity. Sometimes it turns a die-hard believer in whatever it manufactures or assimilates. There is a sense of security in believing. All is well that runs well, but when something tumbles, the mind hits a wall. All knowledge is of no avail, to satisfy its doubts. After the uncertainties fade away from memory, the mind returns to its old conditioning for comfort, and the cycle continues.

This delusion habituates one to bank on the unknown when in doubt. People call it god, spirit, intelligent designer and by many other terms. For many, the unknown has created the universe along with life. It is wrathful when one errs; otherwise its demeanour is benevolent. There are many such attributes one has credited to the unknown.

Does angst disappear with one's holding on to the unknown?

Apparently, angst hides behind the veils of the unknown. Nagging doubts do remain, and there is no fool-proof way to test out the hypothesis of one's own creation. There is always the oscillation between faith and disbelief the mind torturously undergoes. Faith waxes and wanes depending on its supporting or extenuating circumstances. People hold the unknown as a short-cut to satisfy their curiosity. Humans still grope in the dark as their ancestors did millennia ago. Angst does exist.

Total attention opens up doors of objectivity in the organism. To satisfy any anxieties, one need not lean on any crutch. That is because the organism has realised that it is just a figment of imagination, no matter how well its shape is. The crutch is the unknown. It can never be a substitute to the reality of the known which is the organism itself.

The organism does not have to believe in its own existence as it is the known. It knows that belief of the unknown for calming the angst is only a fig leaf of cover for its personal inadequacies. Belief has no reality anymore, and there is no answer to emerge somehow from somewhere. Full attention on the consciousness sweeps the angst away, and one's conditioned answers, as well. The play of angst is just one's mind in entertainment. One needs only to give so much credence to it as a play in one's life.

The Society

Many small steps of individuals contribute to the giant leap of humanity in its collective wisdom. Scientists have accomplished magical things from splicing the atom to landing people on the moon. Unity among people has stood mankind in good stead. The individual merges into society and gives it its strength. The symbiotic relationship between the two has made diverse areas of specialisations possible. It has enriched material progress and propelled agrarian communities to modernity.

Society has also the sheer power of its inertia to influence millions of people. Often, wrongful leaders decide and execute terrible actions. They drag along trains of rightful people, albeit the majority participate unwillingly, affecting the whole world. It now falls squarely on individuals, to cut through the drag of their conditioning. The power of attention is useful. People can become beacons of self-expression in their adventure on earth.

The progress made by humanity is amazing. However, the benefits have not percolated to everyone. The world needs to address that issue on a war-footing for a sustainable level of organisation.

Society has a hand in shaping the overall development of the world. It is amazing how far people have come by in deciphering the magic of nature. Yes, humans were hunter gatherers in the not so distant past wondering at the moon and the planets visiting at night. Now, the collective spirit of wisdom has spread to almost every nook and corner of the world. Individuals are more informed about themselves and the world.

The generations of people have a moral high ground in taking credit for coming this far and accumulating so much knowledge over the centuries. Nevertheless, a lot more can be done in realising the true human potential. Many are still wasting lives in pursuing fantasies rather than turning toward reality.

Society can contribute immensely to individuals. It can give them the freedom to know, develop, realise and evolve to their full potential. Learning and experimenting with life choices are also part of enjoying the freedom. Finally, understanding both the self and society is a single journey as the key to unlocking the one lies with the other.

Reflection

Reflecting on the general state of affairs gives one, both the thrills and chills. It is heartening to benefit so much from the present set-up of the modern world. There is a host of facilities people avail and take for granted in their lives. For example, one can think of: running water, power, sewers, telecommunication, international travel, medical facilities and entertainment. Everyone need not till one's land or hunt for food. Food security implies year or lifelong availability.

Institutions and specialisations in knowledge and services benefit everyone in society. When people share responsibilities and resources, it aids in nation building. Many countries give an opportunity for individual enterprise to thrive. In recent years, even nations come together for big joint projects like space or atomic exploration. All these endeavours have helped humanity remarkably in diverse fields.

On the flip side, only very few people enjoy the luxury of the many modern conveniences the world can offer. To overcome inequality, there is a tendency to perfect existing systems. The results are not encouraging if only one cares to look around the world.

The environment shapes life forms. However, humans have become so powerful that they, in turn, have started shaping up the environment. It is sheer arrogance of humans to believe that the world exists only for them. Their behaviour creates a toxic atmosphere for all living things. People's callous lifestyles result in the extinction of various florae and faunae.

Food, water, energy and other resources from earth are not limitless. People also produce materials, which contaminate the environment irreversibly. Already, there are famine, water-wars and lesser quality of life for all. Future generations will suffer by this wanton destruction. Might is not right. The United Nations reports that more than eighty percent of the people in the world live below ten dollars a day per person. There are still billions without regular food, safe drinking water, sanitary connection or basic physical security. People need food, clothing and shelter apart from being wired for inclusiveness in this knowledge economy.

The billions of poor belong to the third world. Population is one of the main factors for the ills plaguing many countries. The demographic imbalance makes a lethal mix with bad governance, and corruption to fuel world hunger, homelessness, illiteracy and strife. There are seven billion people, social institutions, and accumulated knowledge of the centuries. These assets are enough for all the people to live harmoniously in the world. There are islands of excellence; however, many struggle for existence.

The world is heterogeneous in its march towards development. There are fissures along national, religious, linguistic and several other lines. As a consequence, there is tremendous disparity in terms of wealth, population density, education, governance and a host of other variables. The diversity on the planet makes a truly interesting study. At the same time, it is a challenge, even, to measure its scope.

The dilution of social standards is detrimental to equality and fair play. Corruption and governmental suppression are rampant in many parts of the world. Religion too plays a particularly un-envious role in today's world. The rabid belief of my-god-superior-to yours, legitimises religious conversions and soul harvesting as a tool for subjugating billions. Society cannot wash away its hand when genocides occur on religious, racial or tribal basis. These kinds of horrors still happen with alarming frequency.

Sadly, many people take their own lives in disillusionment. Most often, the state and the public are indifferent to these incidents. It is tantamount to abetment by the society. In addition to these glaring state inactions, one needs to bother about illiteracy, gender inequality, wars and many other natural and manmade disasters. The more powerful always get away with their agenda in conquering the meek in all spheres of activity.

The irony is people have the knowledge and wherewithal to make the earth a paradise for all. Social institutions are several centuries old now. Many such institutions make concerted efforts to change society. Attempts to transform the individual have been going on for ages. The time-tested techniques are through religion, spirituality or even psychological counselling. Despite all these efforts, change is extremely slow to catch up with the demands and necessities.

The world still reels under cut-throat competition, mutually assured destruction, environmental meltdowns, food and water scarcity and skewed development. People fool themselves with entertainment all their spare time. They also hold on to the promise of a glorious afterlife. That is a sequel to all the pain and suffering of the now. If nothing works out, some people escape the humdrum of existence by worshiping Bacchus. The desperate may fall for his newer *avatars* that come with higher potencies.

Many believe in the power of technology to fix all their problems. There are even plans to transfer human consciousness onto robots for gaining immortality. That denouement still may not answer the 'why' of existence. Scientism may be appealing to confused minds. One may expect technology to solve environmental and other manmade issues, but its success remains to be seen. Change is always painful. The countless sages, seers, prophets and messiahs, are powerless to beat ignorance and poverty. Technology or any other crutch can, at best, act as triggers for reflection. The real game changer in self-discovery is the witnessing that makes understanding and action effortless.

Where does one go from here?

The fundamental unit of society is the individual. Humans are seven billion now and may count ten billion soon. If the population were less, resources depleted too would be directly reduced. The ill effects of the chaos could be mitigated faster, and there could be a marked improvement in the quality of life for all. Awareness of antinatalism as a pragmatic policy and its execution for a sustainable population is urgent. It will certainly reduce the negative impact on the environment in due course if sincerely implemented.

People damage the environment by the name of development. To know where one stands is to measure one's situation. For instance, carbon footprints could be an indicator for one's profligacy. Energy guzzling cars, meat industry, deforestation *et cetera* will earn bad points. Reproduction will attract higher points because one more person on the planet will initiate a chain reaction of greater carbon footprints.

Gender-based violence and control are the reasons for a skewed male-female ratio in many countries. The individual and society benefit if they fully understand sexuality and population control. Only when women own their bodies and minds, they are free about their reproductive rights. Then, birth control becomes more mature and meaningful.

Food is a necessity for all living beings. Can the world support a heavy meat-based diet for all its inhabitants? The answer is a big no. Industrialised killing of animals is barbaric and also causes tremendous ecological and health disasters for everyone. To feed the billions of people healthy food, sustainable agriculture is the best alternative. Vegetarianism is apposite for an evolved world. Thankfully, the means and technology exist; but people do not seem to be ready for it.

People must adapt to thwart worse life styles in the future. Sensitivity towards the self and environment is intelligence. Policing alone cannot make people do the right things. Inner control of emotions and sensations through awareness and knowledge can be ways to adapt.

Social Institutions

The organisation of peoples around the world is on the lines of culture, religion, nationality and many such divisions. Institutions and structures are to bring order in one's life. The world today has the benefit of the toil of leaders in various branches of enterprise. Billions volunteer themselves or follow their heroes out of conditioning. The legacy continues with the newer generations, as well. A shakeup augurs well, for people wanting to take responsibility for themselves and the world. Do people have the liberty for a piece-meal approach in restructuring dilapidated social institutions? Alternatively, does the urgency merit a courageous response by living like a leader?

These are questions to be reflected and lived by individuals in complete consonance with their own selves. In such honest engagement, there may be myriad living styles that will prevail in the world. There are rapid changes that are sweeping all over the world. The anchors and institutions of yore are undependable to assimilate these possibilities. Individuals must be free and sensitive to discover themselves fully. Social institutions of the future must cater to the citizen and the group that will foster these changes.

Individuals build social institutions, which in turn mould the newer generations. This process helps to organise people and material optimally. Social institutions have matured over several millennia. They are the pillars on which humanity progresses further in its development. Sharing knowledge and transmitting culture are education. Personally, sex, money and fun are all part of anyone's life. These basic human needs have social institutions like marriage to support them. Humans have a work ethic which is very systematised and interdependent. People have entertainment and sports to cheer up, themselves.

For material development, humans have been studying nature. Knowledge cuts through the morass of confusion and helps one live in clarity. Society should further facilitate developments in science, invest more time and passion in art and, of course, make sustainable evolution for a peacefully governed world. Everyone has a big responsibility towards the fragile environment, as well. The progressive collective responses are the real pillars on which the world stands today. Total attention and understanding in organising the individual and social institutions will create a saner world.

Social institutions have become rigid and are part of one's life. Even a constructive criticism of them will attract immediate repudiation. For instance, going against socially deep-rooted institutions like religion or marriage could invite violent censorship. It is as if social norms have a life of their own, and any contrarian views are unacceptable. People may not be amenable for change. The individual becomes one with society in these situations. They take the law in their own hands defending their rights for the status quo. Both become indistinguishable and individual fury fuels mob frenzy in any provocation.

There may be times to jettison institutions in the wake of some of their processes becoming *passé*. It behoves one freed from inbuilt biases and identification, to realise that. Centuries of conditioning make one hold on to them. Success can be pegged to an objective re-look at one's life. One can then laugh at one's own idiosyncrasies, cry at one's cruelty, be ashamed of one's *naiveté* and also feel proud of one's achievements. Realising the self in the context of society is part of unlocking one's full potential. In total attention, one leverages all one's impressions for the benefit of the self and society.

Family

Family is the socially approved unit for a male and female to run a household, and raise children. There develops a strong bonding in the family when there is love and respect among its members. Parenting is necessary for bringing up children. The child learns the values, language, religion and culture of the family, and it becomes the fountain-head of one's impressions.

A couple brings their relatives, communities and the larger society together, through marriage. Survival, family name, romance, togetherness, commitment, religious obligation, monogamy, heterosexual relationship, parenthood, physical and emotional security, home, social acceptance and identity with kith and kin are some of the ideas that come to mind when one thinks about raising a family.

Marriage is the universally recognized means to support a family, and is held sacrosanct. Matrimony ensures that individuals do not cast away the catholicity of social organisations. Religions do not sanction things, which they perceive, are not of the divine order. All religious traditions accept marriage in one form or the other, though.

The taboo of pre and extra-marital sex haunts many societies throughout the world. Therefore, any dalliance becomes sinful or unlawful and society looks down upon it. Passing on the genes to offspring is intrinsic in the institution of marriage. It implies securing the family name and tradition, as well, for all future generations. All over the world, people accept a man and a woman with their biological children as a natural unit, and there is security for all in that arrangement.

Marriage still rules in the minds of the majority of people around the world and they hold on to the above-mentioned observations tenaciously. For instance, society shuns homosexual couples with designer kids; even though, every child born is a guest of the whole world. Ideally, marriage is a lifelong commitment. The dissolution of marriage leads to separation and divorces. Many a time, people do not break up monogamous relationships due to emotional and societal pressure. People link anarchy with dilution in matrimonial values.

Each family has a personality of its own. Conditioning acts in multiple levels on anyone. Apart from the individuals getting conditioned, family too is constrained to act in a way that society accepts. Just like self-discovery, there can also be a family-discovery, which people can be aware of and introspect. It needs a lot of clarity for the members to work in sync with each other to live in joy and alignment.

When there is openness, one can even redefine the word family to mean a union of people living together as a cohesive unit. It could be a single person or many people sharing their lives in a bond of honesty and integrity. It is imperative to raise the bar of freedom in society which lets the individuals choose their lifestyle without any fear of any prosecution.

Heterosexual marriage is only one of the models of human relationships. Love and commitment can flower anywhere and not necessarily through marriage alone. There are always possibilities for anyone to move towards a universal outlook in friendship, reproduction and sharing, provided there is freedom to do so. Family name is just an idea and not a biological reality. A bastard or a legitimate child carries the same genes from its parents.

Alternative systems are no panacea for the ills of society, though. Full engagement with others requires everyone to transcend the inertia of traditions. It is not as much important to label one's relationships as to be aware of the possibilities of discovering oneself through the same. Self-discovery frees one's mind to accept any healthy type of togetherness among humans as legitimate.

The idea of a family can be expanded to mean the many other possibilities of human relationships. Race, sexuality, class, nationality and any other conditioning lose relevance in the *pot-pourri* of the bodies and minds in the nests people create to live. The union can evolve to provide a sanctuary, and above all an ambience for self-discovery to all the members.

Education

The role of education is so seriously brought out in an ancient Sanskrit sentence; *matha pitha guro deva*. It means after one's parents the reverence needs to go to one's guru or teacher and only then one worships god. Without sharing knowledge, society could not have progressed this far. Education is the link that connects the past with the present and future.

In ancient *Bharat*, *brahmacharis* learnt in *gurukulams*. In earlier times, family skills were hereditary, and that allowed the progeny to learn the craft of their forefathers. Ancient India could boast of university type educational systems, as well, in Nalanda and Takshasila. In today's world, one has schools and colleges dedicated for learning and research in various branches of learning.

Apart from schools, family is also an incubator for learning and grooming of young minds. Along with skills and knowledge, the system passes on many memes consciously and also inadvertently. Teachers share their prejudices and views on religions, ideologies, patriotism *et cetera*. A very glaring example is the hatred against the other taught at schools in many fundamentalist countries. The indoctrination affects citizens, generation after generation creating a vicious spiral of strife all around the world.

Nobody is free from the sins one may commit on children. It is time for a rethink on responsible parenting and educational systems around the world. The youth is the future of humanity. In addition to living skills, they need the freedom to exercise choices, as well, in their lives. In short, elders pass on their scripts, as values and ideals. Children need to be independent to act on their own.

Is there a way to filter out the scripts drilled into the heads of children? In other words, how can adults loaded with so much baggage be impartial in grooming their progeny? First, flush the flotsam and jetsam of one's consciousness.

For that, introspect to know what one truly is. Something may sprout up that leads to a pragmatic response.

Discipline is paramount for education. It will be unreliable if enforced from outside or out of fear of authority. True discipline arises naturally from within, when one is in balance with the impressions. Education is a continual process of learning and sharing. Both the teacher and the taught are in charge for inspiring action. It is not enough to explore methods for livelihood alone. One needs to address the immense possibilities for a life of accountability in an evolving world. The task in sharing this knowledge is challenging as there are billions of people who live with diverse interests and aspirations.

Philosophy

Philosophers and mystics have been talking about the nature of life from time immemorial. The love of wisdom takes one to observe keenly, the way the world works. They based their revelations on altered states of consciousness and supposed oneness with the universe. Some have invoked the divine connection to buttress their claims. Intense moments of discovery abound in the history of many philosophers. Their uttering becomes the final word for many issues. Lineage of seers dots the landscape and timescale of many societies. All these developments have whetted the appetite of seekers to go to the source of existence through their masters.

The fundamental questions of existence are overwhelming. They may pop up in the minds of people who introspect on their true nature. The effort takes on different forms and intensity in one's life. The wise among any society try to synthesise the knowledge of the ages. They stand on the shoulders of the past giants to power their intellect. Knowledge is built on knowledge, by those who toil for the pleasure of wisdom. Some of their analyses of the nature of mind are relevant even for the modern age.

In many eastern traditions, the teachings of the sages pass on through successive generations. That probably explains why, people do not create new gods now. Interpretations of reality may differ, but the goal and *sadhanas* prescribed are mostly universal in theme. The power of philosophy has a tremendous hold on the mass consciousness of the people in this part of the world. The purpose of life may be called *moksha*, *nirvana* or *samadhi*. Beliefs like *karma* and *dharma* are very much part of everyday life. Faith wins over everything else on matters like these and even the uninitiated masses swear by it.

The eastern philosophy gets subtler if one goes by the sages' recordings of their experiencing of reality or proclaimed connectedness to divinity. The *atman* or soul which is immortal yokes with the *paramatman* after a series of reincarnations. *Karma* of the material body dictates its cycle of life. Death is not the finality but only a turning point in the journey of the soul to reach its true nature in the source of all creation. Life is a choice for the individual to accelerate toward the goal of realisation through austerities and *sat karma*. Surrendering to the lord lets one going against all odds. Essentially the spirit is eternal, and the matter is a vehicle that temporarily carries the spirit during life. These are some of the beliefs the majority of the people hold in their consciousness.

People of the semitic books believe in heaven and hell, judgment day after death, sin, and good and evil that govern their lives. They also believe in converting the whole world to their respective faiths. They believe in rewards, in the afterlife if they civilise the heathens in this world. There are many such theories that drive different societies in the world. Apart from the theologians, there are secular philosophers who have tried to explain the various branches of philosophy to the world.

All these philosophical theories could be reactions of the organism to the patterns seen in the world. It could be logical reasoning using certain axioms or emotional surrender to the deity one worships. Society is, by and large, programmed to form moral, legal and ethical standards based on these developments. There are so many definitions of realisation, hopes, beliefs, faiths and scriptures that are prevalent.

Strangely, the fundamental questions remain even after millennia of philosophical enquiry. The cumulative wisdom of the ages does not seem to settle once for all the riddle of existence. In mathematics, the left-hand side of any correct equation equals the right-hand side. One invariably uses the same logic to tackle fundamental issues, as well. The answers are, in fact, the questions themselves rephrased in a different way. It is like going around in circles, like the dog chasing its own tail. It becomes clear that the solution if there is one, lies elsewhere.

There is no need to depend on another person's experience to fashion one's life. There is immense joy to live on one's own experience and knowledge. The courage to stand on one's own feet removes all the conditioning of the centuries. There may be fears of a meltdown of society if people ignore the extant value system. Contrary to those fears, a new world order may emerge that is a bouquet of fresh ideas and sensitive action.

The role of philosophy is to undo one's conditioning through objective study and understanding. It will make people know their limitations, as well as, capabilities. Philosophy will be experiential rather than cerebral in its nature and application.

Religion

Religion, god, and people who claim to be realised have links with one another. Humanity holds god and the few realised ones, important. There is a stamp of divinity associated with a handful of people. The rest are ordinary mortals.

There are many words to qualify a person who is self realised. Some of the terms are enlightened-being, saint, master, prophet, messenger of god and son or relative of god. Some of the religions formed by the holy men are still extant, and others have withered away to obscurity. Prayer and rituals are exclusive activities that are a consequence of religious development. These activities are means to connect the individual with god. Family and society reinforce one's commitment to the ideas and teachings of the religion at birth.

Self-realisation fascinates many people, and there is so much literature about it. Even then, there is no single and clear definition of what it means to be realised. In such a subjective milieu, the hollowness or the sacredness of what the word conveys attracts many interpretations. The idea of realisation has gifted people with a fertile imagination to touch the zenith of existence. Simultaneously, it has also cursed them to be stuck in the nadir of dogma and conditioning. Either way, it invariably leads the majority to a life of incomplete aspirations.

Religions took root on the notions of realised individuals. It has united yet divided mankind. Whole cultures and traditions have sprung up based on the words and deeds of such leaders. Numerous wars have erupted, and millions sacrificed to establish the ideal land. The followers want purity and drive decadence away from earth. The world still functions along the fault lines of religions with such seemingly irreconcilable differences among its peoples.

The power and scope of realisation have been immense in history. It has transformed the way one lives and thinks about oneself. Social laws of today are the culmination of the moral teachings of these men. There are practically no women of influence in the world of enlightenment. The expressions of such insightful men have been a source of guiding spirit for many millennia. The rituals and beliefs have become part of the culture and traditions of societies. People revere those who convince themselves, and the world that they are directly in touch with the source of creation itself.

There are as many expressions of self-realisation as the people who espouse them. This is not to mention the myriads of ideas and thousands of interpretations these teachings have generated. It is beyond logic as to what realisation does to the realised people, in particular, and society in general. People who adhere to a tradition believe that whatever their master spoke is universal in its scope. They zealously try to impose their ideals violently on the rest of humanity, even if, the masses do not appreciate them. Forget the merits or demerits of these teachings, *per se*. It is insightful to trace the evolution of the human narrative in the context of these developments.

One cannot vouch for the veracity of the claims of miracles and supra-normal powers attributed to those ancient men. Herein lays the power of faith in one's life. It is the unshakeable belief in the scriptural texts. More importantly, people fashion their lives in letter and spirit to those words. The hold of these revelations on the collective consciousness is very strong. Even people, who are otherwise rational in their demeanour, fail to question beliefs. The common people lead their lives on concretising faith in the unknown. The sayings and revelations of the realised ones are inculcated generation after generation.

Heaven sends a few mortals for saving people from going to hell. The less fortunate, who are the rest of the world, are to follow the diktats of these realised souls. The followers may be able to claim a piece of the cake at least in the afterlife, if not now. The kaleidoscopic attraction to a supra-human transformation probably keeps people glued to the concept of realisation and its many synonyms. Religion is alive, not yet dead.

Arts, Sports and Entertainment

Arts

Society has institutionalised art to nurture certain innate abilities of people. They produce patterns of human expressions, which attract attention, and imagination of everyone. The medium of art could belong to any sensation or movement, of one's capabilities. In fact, any of one's endeavours can be artistic provided there is a distinct stamp of order and arrangement in it. It turns classy when expressed consciously, and with full attention to both the details and style. All art forms do entertain. Additionally, they attempt to reveal one's innermost self in more detail.

Art triggers imagination. It also creates an ambience to lose oneself in inner silence. Artists witness sensations and creatively express their responses. Matter, sensory signals, words, symbols and ideas are all elements to build art. Any art form showcases knowledge of its creator. Practice sharpens the skill of artists. There are grammar and science in any art form. The effect of art is mainly emotional even though the process of its creation is logical.

Great art can literally sublimate human experience to the realms of another world. It can even kindle and challenge hidden emotions and provoke one's memory. What words cannot convey, a painting or music can achieve. They can move one's heart effortlessly. People cherish masterpieces of art and contextualise them with their own history and evolution. A few of them are timeless and transcend the boundaries of culture, in their relevance. These classics rise above the mundane process of their creation. There are masters who work without any pressure during the process of creation. These gifted artists work from a silent space within them. In such endeavours, they express themselves effortlessly.

Art takes us on a date with one's inner most self. It easily taps into the mental subtleties and helps one in a special journey. The beauty of appreciation lies in the power of sensory signals that nudge one into self-discovery. All Indian art forms speak about this possibility, either through practice or participation. For instance, *nadopasana* is music meditation. The mindfulness of the notes gives the listener awareness of the links between sensations in general and the mind in particular.

People use art for sense indulgence. It whips up animal passion within and attracts more addictions and perversions. On the contrary, if people step back a little to witness and then respond to the sensations, there is peace. Every thought, word or deed, can become artistic in nature and style. Art can free one from the boredom in life.

The voices of opposition to many forms of art and entertainment are getting strident. They represent the fundamentalist mind in denial of the many forms of expression. Conditioning makes people identify with a belief. It pits them against anything, which unsettles the belief system. Even today, many countries do not allow freedom of expression. Artists get brutal treatment from sections of society when they cross any socially accepted boundary. Their work gets regulated according to society's diktats. Freedom of expression is in agreement with progress. In fact, this is a cornerstone in making societies evolve and the world a livelier place.

Literature is the music of language, and music can be the language of literature. They entertain, stimulate and educate people, in more ways than one. There are interesting observations one can make on language, music and attention. A letter or word in language can be likened to a note or phrase in music. Attention, if at all one dares to compare with art, has silence as its building block. Language tries to bring out meaning in sentences while music conveys structures inherent in it. There are certain rules of grammar and idioms for both language and music. Attention, on the other hand, carries an all-encompassing perspective of reality as it is.

Language communicates intellectual processes as much as music expresses emotional content through its rendering. Language can also capture the mood of the moment through description. Similarly, music lays bare the artists' cerebral finesse in their exposition of the same. Essentially language can be used to communicate complex ideas and even precise mathematical formulae. Music can easily trigger associations of memory and emotions much effectively. There is also universality about music, which is appealing. Witnessing is fundamental to the nature of attention. Everything that someone perceives, thinks or acts can be subject to attention.

The skills of both language and music can be taught and defined. The way people have the command over them is an entirely different question, altogether. Attention is natural, and one can at best look at pointers to discover one's true self. Language is an absolute necessity for living in this world, whereas, music takes less precedence. Total attention is very much desirable for a better quality of living. It cannot be defined as one can do so for art and literature.

Sports

Sports can be likened to an art of bodily movements. Any activity in moderation can be invigorating and beneficial for the human body. However, watching sports on television is not going to improve one's physique. People need to commit to shaking up their forms as it is a great way to relax and improve their fitness. Indoor games like chess and scrabble trigger mental agility in people. They also act as fruitful time-pass for old people who are less mobile.

As technology improves, video games and its many versions swoop on the minds of the players, both young and old alike. This is entertainment packed in glitzy gizmos that make people addicted to the games they offer. Parents need to be cautious about the effects of these pastimes on their children. This indulgence works up only the minds of the regular players. Any outdoor activity, on the other hand, provides exercise to the body.

Extreme sports help one to realise the limits of the body and mind. Only the fit and the able-bodied can aspire to engage even in ordinary sports. In many instances, repeated injuries of sportsmen have also caused tremendous physical and psychological damage to their health and well being. The vast majority of people cannot participate in tournaments. In that angle, sport is selective and elitist.

Spectator sports are an interesting dimension of one's social life. It is a marriage of physical activity and entertainment. Winning is the underlying aspect of all games. So is it with one's life. The playing or the sport becomes secondary to the ecstasy of the win. Any sport makes the organism work within its framework. The endurance and tenacity of the body and mind become so pronounced when one stretches very hard.

Sportsmanship is the ability to accept both failures and success gracefully. It is an ideal that needs to be inculcated in children. Knowing the organism, in a physically and mentally demanding situation, requires tremendous attention and training. If there is awareness when one engages in sports, the body becomes a portal to know one's own self.

Entertainment

Modern life centres on entertainment. The world has practically turned every activity into a pleasure movement. People gravitate towards things they like. They use art, literature, music or sports as forms of expression. There is huge money apart from possibilities for the work involved in the entertainment industry.

Entertainment relaxes a tired mind and does titillate one's imagination. It lulls the mind away from worries at least when one is at it. By doing so, it has a major role in calming and civilising people. Entertainment opens up one's consciousness to new ideas and forms. Based on knowledge and experience, one interprets patterns in a show. If entertainment binds one to sensations, it is an illusion. People become bored by being in the gaol of their own making. They look for more and more sensations and get addicted to newer forms of amusement.

Entertainment can sometimes bring awareness of one's conditioning. Then, there is a catharsis, and it is immensely life affirming. Entertainment becomes a life of colours not washed away by the paint. It is a life of music sans drowned in the noise. It is a life of fragrance not wafted away by the odour. It is a life of softness not seared by the rough edges. It is a life of taste not stuffed by the indulgence. As far as the mind goes, it is a life of sublime philosophy, not drowned in emotive literature. People can enjoy the world and whatever it has to offer, in total entertainment.

Science

Humans want to relate to all dimensions of life, scientifically. Science has literally crawled into diverse areas of concern from governance to medicine and computing. It endeavours to find out answers for any question, which is formulated. It does not work towards a result while exploring things; it arrives at results. Science has become the new religion for many. Identification with scientism is again a conditioning, though.

A million words will not suffice to elaborate upon the role of science in human history. Science has been the engine of development from the time of the humble wheel to the lunar mission. Now, it is ready to take baby steps in studying consciousness that has all along been outside its purview. In the process, science carries humans from ignorance to illumination. It is the responsibility of people to translate the spirit of many discoveries to understand one's life better. For example, the pill has overturned the many false ideas about human reproduction.

There are two major spin-offs of science. Firstly, it adds on to the knowledge bank of research and information on nature. It represents and manipulates data for this achievement. In this process, the unknown and its associated conditioning get debunked. Secondly, there is the technological advancement for more comfortable living. There is cutting-edge research in many fields going on in many labs around the world. Technology has a great impact in designing newer machines besides engineering social organisations better.

There is urgency in encouraging people to assimilate scientific temper with experiential reality for a productive and cheerful life. Isolating science from any human endeavour is fundamentalism. Science brings in transparency and universality. It has been able to break many superstitions and taboos through rational discourse. As a result, there is a transformation in the way humans think about themselves and the world. Knowledge is where science is.

Scientists unlock the mysteries of the universe through a reductionist journey. The keys they use are evidence and logic. Life as we know it will be unthinkable without science and technology. The collective wisdom of several generations helps scientists to manipulate matter, energy and information. There are yet, no definitive answers to many fundamental questions of life. They are working hard towards solving many basic questions. The ambition of scientists cannot be castigated as arrogance.

Nature is awesome, and there are many research possibilities. As an example, it is one thing to be astounded by the attraction of iron filings by a magnet, but different to know the cause. This simple phenomenon has urged scientists in developing a phenomenal pillar of the modern world: electrical engineering. Science provides logical and coherent answers to natural phenomena. Additionally, it aids in technological advancement based on the principles of discoveries.

Discoveries in science represent nature in the form of equations and numbers. They are true representations, indeed. Human experience with these things may be far away from the represented knowledge. In some contexts science and self-discovery run parallel courses. The discovery of DNA, for instance, has transformed the understanding of evolution and also one's own body. It conveys that genetically, all living beings are interrelated.

Experiencing reality is a play of consciousness based on knowledge. However, not all discoveries translate into part of one's daily life. How can one experience the physics of ultra small particles of matter or energy and cosmic level manifestations in nature? Quantum mechanics and relativity theory remain just knowledge and symbols. The human brain is limited not to take in all the complexities of nature. Mathematically, the representation of many phenomena may be valid. One's experience need not corroborate with these findings.

The fascinating aspect of knowledge is in its representation and manipulation. Science excels in those schemes. It has a clear goal in deciphering hidden secrets of nature and taming them. Contrary to science, self-discovery neither represents reality nor manipulates it. It has no goal to reach. There is no path, either, as there is no destination fixed. The knowledge and experience one gain can be used as triggers to discover one's position as part of the universe.

The explosion of knowledge can only make one sit up and ponder as to what one is going to do with it. There are choices galore in trying newer and exciting permutations and combinations of all the available information. Are these just means to add more luxury and boost egos in people's lives? Additionally, are they sources to clean up one's impressions, with each path-breaking achievement?

Self-discovery grounds one to observe this juggernaut of information objectively. Then, deciding one's action will not be from a bag of regretful choices. It invariably will be the right action with no anxiety and doubts. Knowledge need not always charge up one's experience about it, and vice versa. It certainly can alter the conditioning that one carries in one's impressions. Self-discovery enables one to witness keenly the play of knowledge, experience and conditioning in one's life. Science propels that wonderful journey.

Commerce

Commerce is a very noble endeavour as it enables the sharing of resources across the continents. A single human cannot survive on this planet. When a group or community gets formed no individual is an island. Interdependence and commerce become inevitable. This innate need for sharing is accomplished through trade and commerce, which spans the entire globe. People manage natural resources by sharing goods and services around the world. Progress is due to the exchanges which have been happening for the entire history of humankind.

Modern life will be unthinkable without commerce and money. The world is yet to see an inclusive benefit for all the sentient beings. There are terrible inconsistencies and inequities within the system. This shortfall will lead people to live in relative bands of purchasing power. The perceived and, of course, actual differences in wealth will be a potent force in destabilising the equanimity of the self and society.

Humans are literally spoilt by the many choices that are available in the world. The stress of not reaching 'there' is a precursor for violence and discord in society. The most basic currency in the material world is money. A no-growth in trade and commerce is not the solution. There are reasons and purpose for sharing in the world. People share for their survival and comfort. Societies, however, get sucked up in a vicious spiral of conflict and mayhem when control is through trade.

Commerce has a direct bearing on the environment, as well. Excesses could lead to a complete meltdown of even the basic necessities of life. Polluted air and water are cases in point. With the current surge in world population, there will be tensions in sharing the wealth among people. Moreover, with unsustainable consumption patterns, the majority will struggle to keep up with the Jones'.

Ecological economics may have to win over neo-classical economics for sustainable progress.

The primary needs for survival are; food, clothing, shelter. One can experience serenity and calm every moment in contentment. Greed forbids one to realise the futility of chasing one's perverted desires. Total attention to situations will bring one's focus on necessities rather than avarice to pomp and show. Everyone benefits if people shed their conditioning for self-aggrandisement. Only then the spirit of commerce will be about sharing, and money will be a tool for progress.

Work

Any effort directed towards an end is work. Work implies time, and one cannot go without the other. There is no work without any activity, either. Traditionally, work is thought of as a means for survival, and also as a religious duty. Activities could be related to the individual or group's survival. Work that helps in one's survival is sacrosanct and purposeful. Personal hygiene, finding food and shelter are a few examples. When one is thus purposely engaged, one can be focused to gain maximum out of it.

Work is the fulcrum on which society functions. Institutionalised work enables people to create goods and services. They get paid or profit in return. Excelling in work requires passion and skills. Money is a major motivation for people to engage in work. Discontentment and greed happen to fuel progress. There is tremendous stress associated with material advancement. No wonder, the world presents a huge dichotomy in the benefits and curses on the way people run their lives.

For the majority of people, work gives self-importance and ways to spend time on doing assigned tasks. Work is both physical and psychological in nature. Everyone does not have the ability to till the land or milk the cows. People need to select work based on their inclinations, talents or opportunities. Industrialists do not slog it out in the farm, but they make millions do so in factories and companies. They chalk out work for the employees.

The world faces enormous rat race and competition. People find that jobs are few and far between to choose. It is common for many people to work on things they do not like. Then, work may become a chore. Exploitation also happens widely, and employees resent it. One compromises on one's life and leads a drab existence. The spirit of winning in the eyes of the world replaces the sheer joy of working. The chore of preparation for action robs off its pleasure. Life becomes more and more cerebral and gets divorced from reality.

If basic necessities for a living are available, what is the motivation to engage in fruitful work?

In total attention, work becomes a situational response. Irrespective of, money name or fame, work just happens. It becomes an unconditional expression of the organism, and the trappings of power desire or reward become absent. Work is not even discharged as duty, and there is simplicity. Great clarity and efficiency ensue from such an operation. The convergence of the needs of the self and the environment find fruition in such action. One is then indifferent to either encomiums or brickbats.

The spirit of perfection can come alive easily in every human being through work. It is an important attitude in life. No doubt, it is welcome to see a job well done. Perfection is just an idea. If one is after it, it is like chasing a mirage. Enjoying work brings perfection. On the contrary, chasing perfection will not make one enjoy work. Perfection, like beauty truth and other abstract concepts are human constructs. Humans have made these ideas part of their conditioning. There could be elements of aesthetics in one's assessment of objects and situations. Nevertheless, superimposing one's ideas of form on to the object of observation is looking for ghosts in the cloud.

Perfecting a skill, executing a task in hand well or pushing one's efforts to the limits are valuable. Indulging in imagination, which is not practical, becomes unproductive. Suppose, a person has an idea of beauty, wherein all the mountains should be of the same height. Then that person must be living in a bizarre world. Perfection as an abstraction creates disharmony in action. When there is the focus in work, perfection follows it like a shadow. Perfect work becomes second nature.

Religions say life is for a purpose. Scriptural texts prescribe activities for all individuals. The gods judge them on this basis for their position in the after-life. The masters tend to colour work as an offering to the gods. For them, life itself becomes work. If people fail in the prescribed duties, they meet a bad ending after death. The promises written in the texts urge people to live literal interpretations of them. For some, even terrorism becomes work.

Once the purpose for life is removed from the conditioning, one's attitude to work will be different. Life has no purpose, as far as one knows. Why complicate it further by finding purpose in work? When people engage in activities like a game, there is great joy. Then the activity itself is the reward, and one need not wait for results or rewards to feel good. Whatever comes out of such enterprise is unadulterated action, devoid of any pressure. Play, in contrast to work is open-ended and fun.

Self-discovery is one such game, where it is a purposeless activity. It could range from scientific studies to commerce or artistic pursuits to global governance. Any activity can be fun, and part of self-discovery by nature. The activity itself is the reward and those who engage in it are totally immersed in the same. The quality of work then becomes highly effective. There is no authority in making anyone work. On the contrary, people do exactly what they want to follow. Self-discovery is never a separate activity or work to know the secrets of existence. Living itself is self-discovery.

Governance

Reflection

Peace inheres in order. Order in society is the fundamental necessity for nurturing humans to their fullest potential. Institutions for governance, law and justice help in maintaining order. Governance becomes the art and science of social organisation that can usher in an equitable world. Otherwise, human resources get wasted.

There can be no orchestra without a conductor. Governance is a tremendous force to control and enforce laws upon the population. Humanity has progressed to this level of achievement because of the power of politics. People in authority not only manage the affairs of their countries, but also negotiate business and diplomacy with peoples in other lands.

Any government comprises of a few people at the top, controlling the people they represent. The propaganda machinery of the state conditions its citizens in various forms. This happens in a democracy, dictatorship, monarchy, communism or theocracy. The state exercises its legitimacy through the government of the day. In many cases, the control is rough, and in others, there are subtle ways, officials play with the politics of power. Individuals who are the basic units of any society have to bow down to this authority. Ignorance of law is no excuse.

The state needs to offer its citizens a million different things from security to growth. Peoples' wants invariably boil down to their freedom of choice. Freedom to think, speak and act is anyone's birthright. Even to enjoy basic freedom, billions of people need emancipation from illiteracy and poverty. Sadly, the bulk of humanity can only dream of liberty in the afterlife.

Whenever there is injustice or calamity, people look up to the state like a mother for assistance. The question that may crop up in everyone is the way to improve upon the statecraft of the nations around the world. One could imagine either an incremental progression or a sudden transformation in the running of the world. Best governance is like chasing perfection. It will always remain an idea in the minds of people.

Drastic changes seem to happen in a country only when there is a revolution or some other calamity. However, a peaceful flowering of governance in any society happens, when it accommodates contrarian points of view and action. Governance has to evolve that lets all individuals express their lives freely. The state needs to transition from being a vengeful entity to an abstraction of openness for all citizens. There one can expect a confluence of action streaming from all individuals.

In today's world, with so much interconnectedness no nation can act singularly without getting affected by events in other places. People are interdependent in this globalised world, and their functioning must reflect that, in letter and spirit. However, hatred based on factors like religion, race, nationalities and language, are endemic. Corruption is another malaise, which is ubiquitous in many societies. It bleeds precious national resources of countries to fatten a few vested interests. These ills still play a role in the lives of the rulers and the ruled.

Ideology and Religion

People identify themselves with their own political ideology, economic interests and religious dogma. A host of other divisive forces also plays a role in defining the way each person lives. The overarching methods of making everyone toe the line of the powerful agencies wreak havoc in the ways societies function today. The inertia is so immense for an individual to effect a course correction.

In dictatorships, any action against the leader will attract draconian laws against defenceless individuals. It is pertinent to note how the religious and other totalitarian ideologies have influenced the governance in many countries, including the secular democracies. The laws and morality of today came from the works of religious leaders. The ancient law givers' writ runs large in many theocratic societies. In many nations, people still accept the words of godmen as their collective conscience. There is resistance to adapt to new paradigms that many a time confronts old traditions in vogue. For instance, even medically necessitated abortions are anathema in some developed countries.

The unholy schisms among various sects and religions erupt into bloodshed, in every corner of the world. Religions do talk of universal brotherhood and love your neighbour as thy self in many forms and colours. In the same breath, they also nurture the 'us versus them' syndrome among their flock, which inevitably dissolves, the universality in their approach. Apostasy and non-observance of certain religious edicts can carry even the death penalty in some countries.

The tentacles of the religious edicts extend even to the bedrooms of people. Adultery in many countries invites execution in the most horrific manner of stoning in public. Many countries enforce religious-based food and dressing habits with an iron hand. Even nations are at war due to these diktats. The list is endless, and it strikes terror and fear in the minds of people all over the world. When people try to enforce divergent views on each other, violence rears its ugly head time and again. Governance takes a beating, and freedom is the casualty.

Leadership

There is a need to muster enough people on a war footing to tilt the balance favourably towards rationality and probity in public life. Fearlessness and courage are consequences of engaging with life totally. Each one of us needs to cultivate clear reflection, objective awareness and selfless adaptation. Trickle will turn into a torrent; individual awakening will turn societies into platforms for allowing people to live according to their true calling. Governance will then be a reflection of the self-empowerment that everyone has a choice to experience.

The leadership is of paramount importance to effective governance. The leaders need to be above criticism and are expected not to be identified with their own personal ideas, and self-promotion. As the Sanskrit saying goes, "*yatha raja, thatha praja",* which means; "as the king, so the citizens." It is binding on both the ruler and the ruled to display commitment to serve justice.

Given the political limitations, it is contingent upon individuals to put the world, not just their community or nation, before the self. This universality in one's thinking can trigger an avalanche of unity and better governance around the world. Self-discovery works magic towards connecting one with the society and also the world.

Defence

Defence has been a necessity for any society from the dawn of civilisation. When a group of people minds their own affairs peacefully, there will always be barbarians who invade and try to rule over the conquered people. Setting up institutions of defending a community is an extension of the survival instinct everyone naturally has. The individual identifies with a society which becomes a nation, and in turn gets security from it. Nations could be formed based on historicity, religion, language, culture or any similarly shared reason.

Control and power of states have reduced the savagery of the past millennia markedly in many places. There was a movement soon after the Second World War to create a world Republic. In fact, no single nation can solve the global issues of today. Nothing conducive is emerging in international affairs that give hope for a nation-less society. One is far away from an alternative world order that could send all the standing armies home. Pacifism is still, work in progress.

The army of any nation calls itself a defence force but that is more in the breach than in the observance. For many, offence is the best form of defence. There is tremendous tension among the neighbours, as a result of one country arming itself to the teeth. Callous selfishness is at play, in defending one's group at the cost of others. People like to win and exert their influence on others. Winning and competition are part of the human psyche. Be it sports, examinations or war everyone wants to win always.

Nations maintain defence forces and flex their muscles through wars to settle scores. They vie with each other for dominance of their people in the world. There is also tremendous competition among them for appropriating natural resources. Clashes often spilling over as wars among nations are inevitable. To confound the fragility in international relationships, there are non-state actors running amok terrorising the world with their ideologies. History is replete with many accounts of wars. Today the horrors of wars are television images in one's living room.

Nothing much has changed from the times of ancient ancestors when it comes to conflicts and wars. There are still millions of deaths and killings in many nations due to the scourge of war and terrorism. National, religious and many other reasons create strife among people. To add fuel to fire the pressures of the ever burgeoning population growth has created chaos in otherwise peaceful states. Land, water and resource wars are common, even within a state, not to mention enemy nations. Policing tries to solve intra-national issues.

Defence expenditure makes the cost of peace high. The nuclear deterrent has in a way prevented skirmishes escalating into full-fledged conflicts. The threat of an atomic holocaust remains hot in many trouble spots of the world. Almost all nations waste scarce resources for their astronomical defence budgets. People live in a culture of war and strife. In fact, conscription and indoctrination are compulsory in many countries. There is knowledge of the futility of war. People have the experience of the brutality that comes with any military intervention. Despite the states knowing these perils, they seldom shed their antipathy against each other. People too are yet to stop baying for each other's blood.

There is an interesting case of the link between war and technological progress. The most horrendous of them all, the second world war belies the common perception that wars stall progress. In fact, there was a surge of creativity and productivity during those difficult times. Almost all spheres of science and technology burst forth amidst the death and destruction of peoples and nations. War brought out the best in people, especially when the soldiers thought they were fighting for a just cause. There was urgency in winning, and there were innovations to get there.

The dilemma is when one knows that the absence of war is not peace. *Shanthi* or peace is not an object that can be leveraged for a gain like progress or happiness. The reward that peace brings along is peace itself. War is not to bring peace. Peace is not to prepare for war, either. The genesis of conflict lies in one's own mind and so is one's quest for peace and order. The apologists are many and strident in war mongering. On the other end of the spectrum, the pacifists day-dream about a world of peace and concord. No wonder one finds both war and peace in the outside world, as well.

One needs to move beyond the duality of conflict and peace. Identification with nationhood can bring upon extreme reactions in individuals. Decent engagements are possible in the world when one wins a war against one's own bloated ego. Self-discovery by the billions may provide the impetus for collective wisdom to root for peace and prosperity. Wars are physical, brutal and bloody. Instead, honest intellectual debates can lead to the right action. Globally interdependent and active people can do precisely that.

SELF AND SOCIETY

Individuals take care of their own interests according to their deliverance. They sometimes make it and most often fall off the mark. It happens in one's health, relationship or even in material progress. Some people achieve greatness in their relevant fields and command respect and emulation from many of their supporters. Right through several millennia, influential individuals have institutionalised certain practises the rest of humanity adheres to steadfastly.

A crying shame in many societies is the lack of freedom for the individual to think, speak and act. Sadly, in various parts of the world governments brutally erase freedom. Collective advancement presupposes individual freedom for all. It should not be curtailed assuming the values set millennia ago. A manageable population with evolved people may be critiqued as a euphemism for, the right quantity and quality of community. Nevertheless, it will turn progress into conscious action, and freedom. How society will turn out, is not for anyone to decide.

The dynamic between the self and society is the key for both individual growth and collective excellence. This bitter-sweet relationship is also part of the total human consciousness. The question humanity has been facing from time immemorial is the right way to organise itself as a group. Even today this is the burning question every society struggles with on a daily basis. There is no magic wand to bring about a formula to deal with this issue. Both religious and secular law can only go so far as to impose a code of conduct for society. A common prescription that has been in vogue as the panacea for controlling people is to bank on the moral laws given by many ancient leaders.

Identification with one's body, mind, family, friends and also the environment makes one protect all these from harm. Altruism may be the evolution's trick in creating interdependence for the survival of the species. Even when soldiers willingly go to battle and die, it is with the hope that at least their group survives. Can humans survive as a people? Unfortunately, they seem to be at each other's throats for the flimsiest of reasons. Thanks to human greed, there is severe pressure for survival for many other species too.

Individually, one responds to situations for one's survival. The many impressions from childhood influence the responses. Collectively, humanity too has institutionalised many things to make society function smoothly. Society has a strong influence and a bearing on individuals and vice versa. Sometimes, there is tension as a consequence. When people play by the rules, they support each other tenaciously. For the silent majority though, society's diktats model their lives. There are inextricable ties between individuals and society. The intriguing bonds are much more than what meets the eye.

Individual behaviour is as much important as societal sanctions are. As an example, slavery was a socially sanctioned institution and very prevalent even a century ago. Thanks to the relentless and courageous actions of a few individuals, this abhorrent practice and collective moral turpitude is history. Just like society influences individuals; leaders too influence society. Individuals turn heroes when they effect change that strikes a chord with society. These are the leaders who have been able to alter the course of history, and one's thinking process itself. However, they are few and far between both in the past and present times. Society has been changing, and there is more access to information in this century.

By the name of tradition, society pushes individuals for an unnatural conformity. The regimentation of living according to plan is making citizens surrender to authority. Alarmingly, that control extends to even one's thoughts and beliefs. Be it in language, dress, looks, and many other traits; many prefer to discard the beauty of diversity to the monotony of uniformity. Culture, religion and the state enforce conformity for easy control of people. Superficially, they may be trying to bring oneness of a nation through these symbols. Nevertheless, in the process, they may inadvertently stifle the independence and flowering of everyone. Being an anarchist and subverting order in society is not going to improve one's life, in any case.

Freedom

The material aspect of existence needs no elaboration. Individuals need to use all their faculties judiciously for greater accomplishment. Similarly, they need to manage all the resources of the world efficiently for an evolved society. Self-discovery enables individuals to know their worth, and also give them the brio to engage with the world more effectively.

Encouragement to the human capital results in progress. Free speech and championing human rights presage better times to come. The internet and other technologies have opened up humanity's mind like never before. In spite of these developments, inclusiveness remains a dream for the hapless in all corners of the world.

Knowing the limitations and strengths, is a reflection of one's capacity. People need to unlock the multifarious links between individuals and society. The reality check will prod one to freedom. When there is the courage to be objective, individuals do their bidding. When one realises freedom, it changes the course set by one's own baggage of scripts.

Freedom breaks the chains of conformity and allows people to rise above their limitations. There is freshness and spontaneity in one's approach to life. Objectivity is not a fantasy held captive by conditioning. Attention gives people, the objectivity to adapt suitably to challenging times. Even a single person's life in freedom will have a profound impact on society. Nobody needs to follow a blueprint for living in freedom. Each one of us can be rooted in ourselves and live in total attention. When everyone acts in freedom and attention, it will not be a cacophony of noises. The society should be conducive for letting billions of voices roar. Mutual trust and freedom between the self and society will then become reality. That will be a new awakening in mass consciousness.

The masters assert that self-realisation and religious commandments are means for eternal freedom. These can make individuals aspire to fit in the mould of their heroes or messiahs. They imagine a state of perfection by doing so. However hard one tries to get into another's shoes, it will not be a smooth fit. The stress to reach the imagined goal will also haunt them. The conditioning, one carries, directs the mind to believe in self-realisation as described by the religious masters. There are not many spiritual explorers who experiment, with their lives, to attain sainthood. Nevertheless, the vast majority leads a life on values taught by their prophets or gurus.

The present century is much different from the times of the ancient saints. Centuries of hypocrisy have gone by, yet, there is no sight of a tectonic shift in its functioning as prophesied by those leaders. Can the ancient ideals still be the blue print in bringing order in the individual and society? To retain or not, is the question. This is not to suggest throwing the baby with the bath towel. On the other hand, it finally rests on the individuals who want to realise their own self-discovery. It cannot be a goal set by someone else that one follows. Life should not be made into a race for attainment. It is to be lived well based on understanding all one's impressions.

Societies do not foster such freedom for many individuals. Culture, religion and several hidden conditioning curtail one's own discovery of life. The mass consciousness in the world is rife with narrow mindedness across sects and groups. Preaching ancient ideals and indoctrinating children are not going to open the doors for freedom. A shake up will make people embrace each other maturely. In fact, collective evolution is indeed the need of the hour.

Perfecting age old systems to fashion modern knowledge-based society, is a compromise. It is not a choice in evolution. No one can destroy history; so blaming the past is not a solution. If better sense prevails, one can avail of the wisdom of both the past and present. One needs situational awareness, take in new knowledge, and adapt objectively. However, the choice of action depends on one's own blueprint.

People need to be aware of the many assumptions they have about realisation. In fact, individuals can have their own self-discovery from first principles. Imitation will not please one's ego in the long run. When one accepts one's individuality, there is freedom from the doubts of existence. The anxiety in becoming someone else gives way to enjoying life in one's own skin.

Collective evolution is not for any ideal to be reached. Ideals and goals have become part of the mass consciousness of people. They are the preserves of the sages and prophets who made them public when seized in their epiphany of realisation. Their realisation might have been genuine for them. However, following it verbatim does not make another person embrace life intensely. It becomes after all a second-hand existence.

Individuals need to get a handle of dealing with the many scripts running within them. There are many socially enforced legal laws, and religiously anachronistic moral laws buried in one's conditioning. Total attention lets one adapt to situations one faces. Use the current knowledge and experience, without any stress to conform to any old ideals. Then, there is the freedom to think out of the box, and act in ways not even imagined until now. This is evolution in action freed from the shackles of conditioning. One need not strive to lead any idealistic life, any more.

People limit their identification to only a few things in the world. The more they embrace the world the more things become part of them. They can connect to the mountains, rivers, people, animals and plants. Just like the various organs within the body work in tandem, people can integrate with the rest of the universe in interdependence. Living should not be with a spirit of competition and exclusivity always. This will usher in a new era of responsibility towards the self and the world as a whole. Survival will then be effortless and an expression of total attention.

The peaceful rise is a possibility for the world, as much as, understanding is for the individual. There is no goal or stage to be attained for either the individual or the collective. No definition can qualify realisation. The conditioned mind can make a thousand definitions of heaven and enlightenment. The spirit lies in the intensity of one's sensitivity to the universe in general, and life in particular.

0: THE QUEST FOR REALISATION

One person's realisation is not another person's salvation. What do people seek and what do they expect to find? People can see that if they map their own consciousness, the Everest, they overlooked all their lives stared at them. There is also the shame in their naiveté in trying to wade through the Mariana trench within their minds. Being watchful of oneself brings clarity. One will neither have to bump into a mountain nor drown in an ocean of hidden things in one's consciousness. The bonus is that, the attention will let one be peaceful, high and dry.

What is the chance for a group of people living in total attention? It certainly is fun, and the world is waiting for it. Self-discovery is not about attaining an object or an idea. Since it is not so, it has zero attributes and no feel to it. When there is a realisation of the process of seeking, self-discovery ceases to be a state of achievement.

Realising how one lives is necessary to uncover who, one is. There are causes for one's response to situations. Being aware of the processes helps one to use all one's capabilities. Behaviour is the result of conditioning and environment in one's life. Every child gets food and culture for its body and mind respectively. No wonder, there is a struggle to break free from behaviour or any established social mores which one may resent.

People most often make a tangled web of their lives. Happiness or some other emotion cannot bring respite from the reality one loathes. No one can choose the environment of their liking. At best, they can witness situations and their responses. In that space, people can understand their deep held ideas and beliefs. Then it becomes easy to extricate them from the mess of their own making. Every moment is practicing time.

Living is easy sans the pretences and falsehoods one unconsciously follows. When one is conscious, there is vitality to know what one truly wants and live accordingly. There are pointers all over in this intriguing self-discovery. Life bestows a chance to be synchronised with oneself and be sensitive to society, world and the universe. Realisation is not an ability to be better than others. It is an individualised awakening. Since it is not a skill or booty, there cannot be any definition to it. Total attention opens up vistas for individuals to express and adapt to the changing times. Life becomes a privilege and responsibility.

THE SEEKING

What is seeking? Even knowing fully, that the object of search is nothing but the figment of one's own imagination, one seeks. One learns from infancy, to nurture a faith to see the lights of heaven. In daily lives, one sees cause and effect in operation. Why should one think otherwise in matters of the unknown? The godmen have expressed the unknown, in a language known only to them. Their sense of morality has cloistered people to hold on to the idea of eternal freedom. The godmen have emboldened themselves to rationalise that people can metamorphose into superhuman beings. The benediction is true, if and only if, people obeyed them. People submit themselves to the godmen as part of their religious duty. They follow the commands implicitly and maintain dress codes, food habits and rituals. Heaven is after all just a step away if they pay these small prices. Could one ever emerge from the forest of delusions to one's own field of the known? It is an illusion to dream reality.

Angst provokes seeking. It could be the mystery of life that nudges one to find the source of creation. Humans have been working hard to unravel the secrets of nature through science. Beliefs too make one seek what is in one's own mind. There is a need to fathom the hidden workings of one's deluded self, as well. Whenever inadequacy haunts people, they seek the unknown. On the other hand, if one has faith in one's supernatural ability, it is an unassailable proof of the mind in denial of its own limitation. It requires courage to call, a spade a spade. That conviction comes only through understanding oneself.

The inquisitive mind wants knowledge of everything it surveys. Only then it can control its *objet d' desire*. Once it gets a handle of that, it moves on to the next object. Initially, one might be tempted by bliss or enlightenment from seeking realisation. When the seeker fails repeatedly in getting and maintaining their imagined state of beatitude, they surrender. It dawns only on intense seekers that these are ideas, after all. Seeking indeed seems to be a Sisyphean act. Nevertheless, when one strips off the expectations from seeking, what remains is the equanimity that comes along irrespective of one's situations in life.

One normally gets motivated to work for gain. The mind even objectifies realisation and makes seeking a method to achieve its goal. Some people dedicate themselves, seeking realisation. Seeking cannot be prescribed as work at all. When people institutionalise it, they have again made an exotic occupation. Life becomes regimented if one defines and works towards a state of desire. People cannot observe situations if they wear blinkers for achieving realisation. Individuals lose the freshness of their own lives in such torpor.

There are as many paths to the realisation as the number of people living in the world. In the same breath, there are as many answers to existential questions as the number of questions posed. Every person's realisation is unique. The anxiety, or rather the incompleteness in one's life urges one to seek. Thus, one person's answer or revelation cannot be a panacea for all. It cannot and should never be forced on society; however, abstract and universal it may sound. It is for people to be aware of their own relationship with creation.

Realisation cannot be codified as what the seers and prophets said. In fact, they stood out from the crowd and had the courage and conviction to traverse their own path. The masters also shared their experiences with the world. At best, the uttering of those people can act as triggers for people to discover themselves and live responsibly. It is imperative to break free from imitating others on such matters. It is only the remnant of a master's living pattern that one can follow.

A question may crop up as to, who is the realised one. There is no way anyone can get a certificate of realisation. As long as the mind craves for an unknown state of enlightenment it is in perpetual denial of reality. The desire to be other than one's own self is a recipe for sorrow. Seeking for anything else than what is possible is fantasy. People try for an inner transformation to happen. They label that as a state or the realisation that is to be achieved either now or in a future life. Seeking persists, as long as, there is hope and demand within to be supra-human. The mind believes either in miracles or in efforts to achieve its own paradise that it has created.

This is not to suggest that one should not try for change, growth or improvement in one's living conditions. Change alone is permanent, and one is part of that flux. Realising from the basis of the known rather than any idea of the unknown makes the seeking logical. One is very much rooted here in the known and need not grope in the impressions that one has assimilated about the unknown. Seeking the source of existence then turns into joy. The deliberations are not about propping up atheism, agnosticism or theism. Enquiry from scratch is neutral.

The Compensation for Seeking

Is realisation the compensation for seeking?

Human life abounds in transactions. There are no free lunches in this world. Even in relationships, it is, 'I scratch your back, you scratch mine'. On the contrary, nature is just neutral. The sun shines irrespectively of what one thinks of it. Everything in life spins on compensation. A give-only-when-I-take attitude is hard-wired in the brains through nurture. If people want a child to stop crying, they offer a chocolate to it. A rose stem could fetch peace from one's angry sweet heart. The list includes even one's relationship with the divine. In religion, the least one can do is to praise the lord, if not contribute to the religious institution.

Some other facets of life in terms of, cause and effect, are common knowledge. If one does not take adequate care of one's body, it fails. If plants are not well nourished, they will wither away fast. The same happens with a career, as well. One knows how important transactions are to any business enterprise. Society's diktats are to be followed or people get ostracised.

There are subtleties in handling one's mental faculties. Calmness douses the fire of anger. Reassurance erases fear.

Hurt needs love to repair. Rejection calls for acceptance. Even emotions seem to need a balance, or they may fly off the handle. One compensates a loss with the sensations of a gain. For instance, when people are broke or fail in a relationship some may turn alcoholic. The new sensations of the drinks are to heal the previous hurt. Handling success too could lead to stress. Unconsciously, people seem to balance the lack of a set of sensations with another. People are unable to accept sensations as they are.

The old saying, 'what you sow, so you reap', is one of the basis of morality. The cause-effect theory or *karma* too claims to explain many of life's unanswered questions. Reflecting on these subtle processes make one aware of the conditioning to compensate for each and every activity. People need to free themselves from the long chain of bondage of their perception. The irrationality to compensate for everything one thinks, feels and acts is tiring.

Adopting the same attitude in self-discovery, as well, turns seeking into a counterpoint to the trap one feels in one's life. It could be the pleasure people search to offset the pain in them. Otherwise, it could be a balancing act for one's intellectual curiosity. The seeking as a catalyst mutates the quest or idea of realisation into a new belief which one swears as truth. This involves effort and time. Again, the result is of the same material with which one started one's journey. One is back in square one.

Is there a way to break the impasse? If one deconstructs the above written text to find a way out, one can sense the absurdity in pursuing any method to achieve realisation. The method is just a compensation to win something tangible or ideated. The awareness of one's nature frees one from wanting to compensate the non-compensable. Life is neutral!

When one is clear in mind, action is a natural expression. It is not a reaction that compensates for an earlier action, either now or in the afterlife. One can experience that in complete attention, duality, *karma*, *dharma*, nature and life are not things to be compensated. They are to be witnessed at every moment. One needs to be consciously in tune with oneself. The toil and moil to make good a loss or to become something new will be history.

The Unknown

The seeking of the unknown is due to a belief in its existence. Many hold faith in attaining it, somehow, through religious practices or spiritual techniques. The religious swear that if not for this life time, salvation is around the corner, at least, after death. It comes with a rider; one's present action and even thinking determine one's future status. Thus, the seeking and the unknown are two sides of the same coin. If one dissolves, the other too vanishes.

Science expects the evidence to validate new knowledge. On the other hand, faith presupposes the unknown as an axiom on which everything rests. Faith-based activities and attitudes are tethered to the lives of prophets, messengers, saints and gurus. For the faithful, the inflated stories of their heroes are enough evidence for the unknown.

Realisation turns colourless and dissolves in many shades of grey, when the masters proselytise it by the shadow of the unknown. Realisation from the position of the known, on the contrary, is colourful. It animates lives much more than what the twins, the seeking and the unknown, promise to provide for eternity.

Life, Death and the Unknown

Of the many things which are unknown, death is a reality which defies any logical explanation. Questions like, what comes after death and the very nature of death itself fuel one's angst about the unknown and also the unknowable. Everyone goes through the grief and pain when a near and dear one dies. Society bears witness to death in many grotesque forms and numbers. All such natural and wanton tragedies trigger anxiety and anger in people.

Taxes and death are here to stay. Animals, unlike humans, do not kill each other except for food, and rarely for territorial control. Shockingly, humans have industrialised killing to humungous scales. Ageing, terminal diseases and environmental calamities are natural and unavoidable. There are many manmade issues, which are certainly avoidable. They may be due to political, national, judicial, religious, social and even personal causes.

Politically, death is a weapon that both the state and the non-state actors employ to intimidate and control their enemies. Nations settle scores through wars and the pain of mass murder. Society extols killing as a valiant deed if the soldier happens to be on the right side or despised if he is from the enemy camp. In many nations, law demands the use of the death sentence to bring justice to its citizens.

Life and death befuddle people. To counter that, they have come up with myriad possibilities for immortality. Many philosophies can be traced back as attempts to solving this mystery. Religions have invented heaven, hell, afterlife, liberation and other goodies to perpetuate life forever. They promise paradise provided the devout stays committed to the cult and its teachings. If not, the teachings instil the fear of hell for disobeying the diktats of their founders. Entrapment of people with such dire consequences is the age-old technique of using death as the key to controlling societies.

Suicide is one of the most difficult existential issues to comprehend. The suicidal person shortens life so as to escape the realities of life one dislikes. The mind exercises its power to override even survival instincts. The cases may be few and far between, but the numbers are quite sizeable than meets the eye. Depression and other mental illnesses are the major causes for suicides. The body cannot initiate *hara-kiri*. Mental processes, though of the body, influence one to take the fatal decision. This aberration is unnatural. Through this, the organism protects itself from perceived suffering in the future. The unknown death seems to be less harmful than the known anguish. A suicidal person banks on the unknown in favour of the known misery. The organism loses its situational awareness and resorts to this final step.

People with chronic pain or artificial life-support system may want to terminate their suffering. There is a tradition of ritual starvation sanctioned by many religious orders in India. Old and ill people withdraw from society, and meditate before embarking on this path of no return. They chant mantras and partake of only water. Some refuse even that in this ritual of welcoming death. The organism is again protecting itself from probably prolonged and worse states of deterioration than this rite.

The body itself wears away if left to itself without any nourishment. Prescribing euthanasia as a one-shot remedy to beat suffering is institutionalising a custom. One needs to take decisions without any biases of the conditioned mind. Suicidal thoughts may sometimes be a trigger to find the nature of reality. Realising the subtle mental processes could be a catharsis in doing the right action.

Can one ever get to the bottom of what it means to die?

The mind has a tendency to analyse and remembers events as milestones in one's life. The experiences become one's life story. Without them, life bears little history. Birth is an event, and so is death. When any change happens, it is an event. Stillness or peace cannot be events. One cannot recognise ageing or the gradual decay as a harbinger to death. People only react to events, which are sudden shifts from the status quo.

If one starts to recognise death as a process which kick-starts itself at birth, one's approach towards it will be more mature. Death and life are twins that exist together. Death never opposes life. On the contrary, they function together. They are two possibilities for a being at any point of time; being alive or dead. At the end of one's time on earth, both death and life exit together. Death too vanishes with life. Death is an event that defines the organism's inability to adjust with the internal and external environments. At that critical juncture, both the potentials of life and death leave the organism.

Logic or emotions only represent one's knowledge through words or art. The mind at the most can play around death but cannot experience it. Being open to the processes of the organism, one can accept death unreservedly. It helps to transcend one's dismal view of duality of life and death. The tragedy of the world is nobody cries for the death of the unborn. If only, humans care for their future generations, the world would be a better place. Realisation is not a skill to know or alter any of the life processes like death. In being less identified with the ideas of death, one can mitigate the fear and uncertainties that hover around its mystery.

Expression of the Unknown

People express their feelings about the unknown through language or other fine arts. It is insightful to ponder over such an outpouring that is said to contain divinely and out-worldly truths. Scriptures and similar books or messages of the masters base their theories on the unknown. People who claim to have reached the acme of perfection try to describe their experience through discourses. Language is of the mind, and so are the expositions describing their angst and its solution.

Suppose everyone comes with a tangible dimension higher than the known. People may tilt towards that and be indifferent to the angst in their minds. Otherwise, it smacks of one's imagination of the unknown, and also an unbridled enthusiasm for out-of-body experiences. One needs to be conscious of one's own mind clearly to solve this puzzle.

The mind has a form within which it functions. People try to peep out of this wall around them and express their experience. Language cannot be a tool to describe the unknown since it too falls within the confines of the mind. Mystical language talks of the wonders without the boundaries of the mind. This is nothing but imperfections of the language that tries to convince people of the dimension beyond the mind. In fact, the unknown forms in the foundry of the mind itself.

People fall trap to the imaginings of the collective mind that has been developing over several millennia. The legacy of the collective mind holds the seeds of one's imagination. It could sprout out the contrived shape of the unknown. The unknown tries to fill the lacunae with one's objective reality check. In witnessing, there is a choice to bask in one's own understanding. Then one can realise who and what one is without a tinge of any unabated angst.

Witnessing enlightens both the form and the content of the mind. Both of them are, after all, the processes of consciousness. In such transparency, there is no scope for the unknown to remain a veritable esoteric dimension either within or without the mind. The unknown finally gets exposed as words, ideas, beliefs and one's own conditioning. The known pares away the ideas from one's mind leaving vibrancy and clarity in life.

Godmen for the Unknown

People in large numbers defend their respective spiritual or religious identities. Conditioning and indoctrination from childhood could play a major role in this phenomenon. There is also widespread belief in the power of god and godmen. They seemed to have willed out a destiny for religion in accordance with their words and action. One needs to acknowledge the hold of the divine on the hearts and minds of people.

The thinkers of the world have always grappled with two important questions—origin and organisation—of life. Many godmen speculated on human origin and propounded certain guiding principles to organise society. People even draw parallels between current science and their masters' revelations aeons ago. They can validate their books and be religiously and politically correct. Many theocracies bear testimony to this.

The words of godmen of yore have power upon the people; their wisdom inspirits into the collective consciousness even today. It certainly was a man's world, and there had been severe restrictions on the equality of men and women. That is why one does not find any woman prophet or master anywhere in the world. Misogyny in religion still holds sway in many parts of the world.

The godmen have explained sublime things like the origin of the universe to mundane things like proper eating and dressing styles for their group. The words were god-centric with a certainty and vehemence which are hard to brush aside. This seals the scope for negating them without incurring the wrath of the custodians of faith. Faith and the faithful complicate the simplicity and grandeur of life by defining these in their own way.

Society has always been tame enough to accept their writ and decree throughout the ages. In the ages with no modern communication, it is fascinating to note how the fear of the unknown spread among people. The fear includes death, the wrath of the gods in the now and afterlife, and mysteries that cannot be rationally explained away by anyone. The very unknown happens to be the tool of the godmen to root for their position. Naturally, all the definitions turn Arcanum to everyone else.

People dislike thinking of themselves as orphans in an orphaned world in an orphaned universe. They try desperately connecting with an imaginary source of creation. When they fail, they blame it on their sins and faults. A few men say they are from the source itself. The majority follows them like lambs led to slaughter. It is a travesty of truth and murder of integrity to claim superiority over fellow humans. Additionally, they load guilt on them and put the onus on the hapless followers for their insignificant lives. The religious leaders lead people to believe in a promise of salvation that no one can deliver. Unfortunately, people base their lives on the words of these so-called realised men. The words they claim are from the unknown and are the genesis of conflict among different communities.

The effect of those uttering has a significant impact on the development of religion, culture and society. There is nothing to either condone or condemn, in the birth and trajectory of such thought processes. It is imperative to understand the nature and tenacity of one's subtle conditioning. Individuals are at a crossroads now in deciding to either dig their heels deeper in superstitious beliefs or to evolve based on the clarity of the known.

Locating east needs a reference point of the sun. If one is in deep space out of the solar system itself, where is the question of east or west? One can deduce that without reference, faith is shaky, and belief turns into dismay. Realising one's consciousness will be a case of touch-and-go when the unknown is the reference point. In other words, when one refers anything to the unknown, it causes disarray. Observing and accepting things from a relativistic frame work of the unknown are subjective. Contrarily, understanding is unassailable and objective when one can vouch for it from the position of the known.

Morality of the Unknown

Godmen have been teaching that altruisms and ideals are attributes of the unknown. Moral values are the bedrock on which they command people to run their lives. By doing so, they hope to create an ideal world. There are pockets of excellence, no doubt, but by and large, the world is a terrible place for an ordinary person to live. Survival itself is tough and unpredictable.

Altruism cannot be at the cost of knowing one's own true nature. It is the ego which trumpets altruism as something superhuman. Society, extols these sacrifices as immaculate, and also makes people practice them. Any act born of such prevalent notions of idealism need not be spontaneous. People lose their originality, and they become cheap imitators. Humanity has institutionalised these in many forms. When ideals dictate lives, it smacks of relying on the unknown for society's future. The ideal of the unknown has spawned more arms race and divisions than creating paradise here on earth. Chasing a goal of an ideal society is imagination at work that makes one hope for a better future.

People have been breaking their heads for millennia to get precise definitions for ideals like truth, beauty, love and justice. People give different meanings to these, which are vulnerable to infinite interpretations. There are naturally differences of opinions that crop up in describing and living by these ideals. Physical fights and violence are rampant on these counts. Where actual fights are under check by force, psychological turmoil upstages them to vitiate the whole environment.

Individuals can witness their uniqueness when they do not submit to the unknown. The fixation for expanding affiliations of one's sect is herd mentality. There is commonality among humans that are beyond the superficialities of name and form. People need not idealise any abstract concept for building relationships. Many people with an independent attitude to ideals in life will have a domino effect on society. There will be sensitive interaction among people freed from the shackles of enforced morality. The freshness in individual awakening will overcome the complexities of bringing inclusiveness among people. One can depend on the known to open the doors for expressions, which are hitherto impossible.

Hold of the Unknown

One knows in a small corner of one's heart that certain things are unknowable. Nevertheless, the quest goes on to get to the bottom of existence. There is no light at the end of the tunnel. People need a semblance of fullness in their lives. They hold on to a device of their own making—the unknown—a construct of the mind in its frailty. People call it by different names like, god, spirit or soul. Apart from these grandiose ideas, fears and angst can also be clubbed to this variable. The supernatural, angels and demons too are part of this. Even astrology is searching for the unknown future.

Many an unknown comes to the realm of the known through rational discourse. There are still various imponderables unaccounted for in life. The mind has no other recourse other than hanging on to the unknown for comfort. It does so tenaciously and adamantly. The firm believer infects other minds viciously by transferring his creed. The godmen and prophets have done exactly that in spreading their own ideas of the unknown so fanatically.

The unknown is in the imaginary landscape of billions of people worldwide. Everyone may have an opinion of it. People would have read or heard about it from scriptures or folklore. Now the unknown is an axiom; an unshakeable faith in the pit of conditioning. It is a legacy of culture, history, civilisation and tradition. There is nothing wrong or right about it. It is surprising that the known, which is knowledge in clarity and experience, projects an illusory unknown to satisfy its own curiosity. The mind lulls itself in apparent total knowledge by filling its holes with shadows. It cannot hold water for long. People, however, learned or experienced, still carry doubts.

The unknown plays such an enigmatic role in people's lives that it is important to be aware of its extraordinary force. The known creates the unknown and masquerades it as true knowledge. It cannot get more trivial than identifying with this mind-play. The known alone brings more clarity in one's engagement with the world.

Freedom from the Unknown

Defining realisation as an object stems from the mind. It always wants a source for everything to feel complete. It needs to know, control and possess the realised state that it has objectified. The mind has turned the self into an idea or worse an abstract entity residing in the body. Then it feels that it has realised the self. The mind wants to experience the realised state which it has created. It then tricks itself to feel elated when it has a semblance of its imagination. The mind tries to link the effect of being in such a state to the nature of realisation itself.

One is alive and can comprehend the known from the impressions one has been gaining from childhood. The idea of attaining the unknown, which is something other than what is, causes restlessness to seek that. Realising this simple nature of the mind brings peace. The calmness underlies the veneer of all the doubts one constantly churns up. This understanding can take root and flower within everyone. For this, there is no need for any external crutch; be it, any individual or their ideas of self-attainment. In fact, the ideas are only impediments to one's catharsis.

Many people look up to the unknown to bring order in self and society. It is in a way shirking the responsibility to know oneself and act accordingly. Any spiritual outsourcing to someone else's will, often ruin people's lives. Submitting one's freedom to anyone or anything is akin to casting away the opportunity to know oneself. No one puts effort to cognise that one is alive. Similarly, realising one's consciousness is effortless. Step back a little, bring in attention, be conscious of the mind, have awareness and let clarity and objectivity rule; to feel at ease in any situation.

When the known is the basis for leading one's life, living takes a giant leap forward. One may feel vulnerable to accept the inability to know the totality of life. In fact, this is liberating than holding on to someone else's description of reality. There is, at least, honesty and independence in one's existence. Individuals can adapt based on their own understanding and act right. It depends on the times, knowledge and circumstances in which they live. Even, *dharma* need not be lines cast on stone. Societies can benefit only by the blooming of courageous citizens who stand on their own.

Realising the known thus gives freedom from the hold of the unknown in one's life. There will not be clashes between the ideas of the unknown among different torch bearers of many communities. When everyone works from the basis of the known, dissemination of information is easy. It does not rely on metaphors, symbolism or poetic meanderings as is the case with the unknown. Even when people have to entertain thoughts of the unknown, they can fathom the ways their minds work. Briefly, understanding is of the known and imagination is of the unknown. It is up to people to decide where they want to be. It is their choice.

THE 3M

An ounce of practice is equivalent to a ton of theory. This script which is as old as the hills rings out loudly whenever one looks toward experiencing what one learns. Even realisation is not exempt from this temptation. One always tends to associate an experience with a form, sensation or an idea. When the Eureka moment does not happen with realisation, there is bitterness in the seeking. One expects sound and lights, and a liberal dose of divine connection; sadly, it evades such a climax. Is it an anti-climax or a damp squib, especially after a long and prosaic journey to capture it?

Leaving the semantics apart, it is conditioning that makes one want a spiritual orgasm. This conception grounds one back to reality irrespective of one's spell with realisation. In this journey with neither a path nor destination, a few shows on the side entertain and keep one going. The 3M techniques point out that people are the tools, hoping and struggling in desperation to become the masters of their imagination.

The 3M stands for Map of consciousness, Mindfulness and Meditation. These are practical exercises for the mind and brain that can fetch far-reaching insights to the practitioners. In recent years, many scientific studies have attested to the long-held beliefs in resting the mind for health benefits. Modern imaging techniques have found out that the phenomenon in question arises due to the neuro-plasticity of the brain.

These techniques can alter thinking and also the structure of the brain. The research claims that there is a reduction in negativity, and enhanced well-being of the subjects. One needs to be open enough to know one's own consciousness better. The little mental tricks affect the one who indulges in them. The mind plays host to jealousy, anger, happiness, and other emotions both good and bad, day in and day out. Half the solution to any situation is in knowing the problem fully. These types of contemplation do precisely that.

Map of Consciousness

Introspection

Introspection, in normal parlance, means looking into one's own consciousness. Literally, and figuratively, one's life is the result of the body, mind and society. These things are tangible and with the right focus discernable. Introspection reveals one's likes and dislikes, for a start. Then the identifications with one's ideas get clearer. Even when one gets carried away by emotions or fads, introspection brings one back to *terra-firma*.

Reflection is a way to know one's own consciousness. Silence is the mirror to do that well. Mapping of consciousness bares even the many hidden things in one's mind. The conditioning, blocks, genius and potential get a breather in one's attention. The mind is the only thing which can know itself. Watching the mind sans judgment is essential for a stress-free life. Focusing on sensations and the mind illuminates the dependence of one's desires and sensual pleasures. This self-reflexive action or introspection makes one aware of the patterns of thoughts that conditioning generates.

The more intense one's power of observation gets the better is the self-discovery. This process is not to be confused with a behavioural self-study. In day dreaming, one falls into hallucinations or fantasies of the mind. While introspecting, one needs to be specific about the problem in hand. It gives a clearer picture of the issue from all angles. There is acceptance without regret or anxiety of any genuine action.

Disquisition

Disquisition is a careful analysis of any problem with another person or a group. It is a powerful way to unravel one's own mind. The other person or group acts as a mirror and makes one's stand clear. It requires patience, empathy and non-judgment to open up a true dialogue. Apart from all these traits, one needs a spirit of unflinching impersonality to take the talks forward. People can discuss anything under the sun.

Genuine enquiry happens in *têtes-a-têtes*, when the participants listen to one another. People have a tendency to defend their egos during deliberations. The group in disquisition should be careful, not to slip into a verbal duel. The dialogue is not reality because the moment something gains a tag it loses its absolute position. What it probably does is to nudge people to look into themselves without any fear or bias. In such an intense engagement, words lose meaning and what remains is silence to know oneself better.

Meditation and disquisition can go hand in hand to reflect on one's consciousness. Let one add a bit of caution here. Talking and discussions with an equally inclined partner or group will be beneficial. There is no point in a mental gymnastic session with anyone. It could be a drag and may take one off a tangent. Look out for disquisition when one fully dissolves with a partner of a similar temperament.

Romantic love holds a fascinating key to know one's own self. It is a highly transformative trigger to get to know many emotions deeply embedded in one's mind. Impassioned enquiry happens if ego clashes are less, and suggestions are not personally aimed. In this relationship, one can intimately experience one's body and mind in a truly serene way. Love evolves and matures to bring out the self-knowledge that is ever present with everyone. The whole gamut of life, sex, birth, body and relationship find excellent scope for disquisition and enquiry in this bond.

Realise the infinite ways one can know one's self. It need not be limited to any preconceived idea at all. Reflecting on one's relationship is an unparalleled opportunity to unlock one's consciousness. This can be extended to a group which has camaraderie to enable participants to know themselves. A society too can adopt a genuine discourse for its development.

Mindfulness and Meditation

Mindfulness is exclusion of everything else other than what one attends to at that moment. Meditation is the inclusion of everything that one perceives. It may seem contradictory, but in its truest sense both are qualities that spring from consciousness. The spirit is to be in focus of what one is thinking and acting. Have one's attention focused on the smallest unit of work in hand and at the same time look at life holistically. When one is mindful in all one's actions, it culminates in a subtle yet profound awakening of one's own nature. People cease to be automatons whose behaviour depends on their conditioning. This knowledge through the power of self-awareness can bring calm and peace to one's life.

One can recount the experience of mindfulness while exploring one's own selves. The only thing that one can call one's own is the body-mind complex. The way to discover is through the portal of one's own body and mind. The hunter is the hunted. This may make the hunt very intriguing. Do not define what one gets out of all this. The game itself is enjoyable and is in no way different from the discovery.

One may think it is a red herring to go on a hunt without defining the goal. Once one defines a goal, one is going to recreate the goal within the mind and later achieve it, by hook or crook. Say, the goal is heaven, or for that matter, even self realisation; one will next create a conception of heaven or self realisation and achieve it through visualisation.

The prize becomes one's own creation. One will also fanatically believe in reaching somewhere. This delusion will go on until one feels inadequate again. Later, it is back to square one. This time, it is going to be another goal of permanent bliss. The cycle will go on forever. Defining a goal and fooling oneself for some time till the bubble bursts is not a solution. It will not take one far in the hunt for self-discovery.

Mindfulness is witnessing without fixing any goal. One starts with no baggage and embarks on a journey which is light and easy. There is joy irrespective of what is around or inside one's self. It is a great privilege and joy to experience the serendipitous discoveries one makes in this journey. Then there is the realisation of no destination other than a life in sanity and reality.

Meditation cannot be forced upon oneself. Just like people set the bedroom nicely for falling asleep, they can set their minds calmly to dissolve in meditation. Still, witnessing can function along with any action. In such a state, the organism acts effortlessly under any circumstance. The conscious state, which includes thinking and acting, becomes a natural expression devoid of any wilful interference from past impressions. Living becomes meditative and is in tune with the world.

Mindfulness of things, people and mental processes, could act as triggers for self-discovery. The following methods of looking into the elements, the form and the baggage one carries are powerful and always within one's reach anytime and anywhere.

The Elements

Life is not independent; it needs necessities for its manifestation. The elements are space-time, matter and energy, information, environment and self-awareness. People take for granted the role of necessities in their lives. Reverence and care for these elements are a thing of the past. Exploitation of these resources is the basis for development now. Having a heart for the environment is to go green in the future. Having a head in utilising these resources is to go clean. The elements trigger sensitive beings to act responsibly. Mindfulness of these elements could also be the attention to one's own body. In fact, without them, no one can take a form and live.

There is no escape from space-time matrix. It passes right through one's body.

No one objectifies space as it never resists any movement through it. Space is light and empty, even though, scientists talk of dark matter in it. Luckily, humans are yet to manipulate or destroy it. One can design buildings that can ingeniously use space and the environment to one's maximum advantage. The layout of cities and architecture tell a different tale in many places. Now, urbanisation is about making a concrete jungle. Connectivity is about building highways searing through pristine forests. Homes and offices are claustrophobic to the majority of humans. The list is full of the many blunders with the environmental damages in recent history. The result: one forgets that one is part of space, sky and the celestial magnificence.

Thanks to the ocular perception, one can visualise two disparate dimensions; the cosmos and the quantum world. People's awareness and perception do not change the objects they survey in the day-to-day world. To measure space one needs instruments. Nevertheless, the brain can imagine the sizes easily. If one were to shrink to sub atomic levels, the quantum environment looks as complex as the universe one watches now. Before the Big bang, the potential for forming the universe was probably present within that *bindu*. Nothing can exist, move or be part of the universe, if not for the spatial dimension. The wonder of space makes one appreciate the grandeur of nature.

Life is so hectic that people do not think about time in their lives. Time is like electricity. Use it purposely or lose it. However, whether one uses it, or not, time like space is never absent in one's life. Life is a function of time and occurs between one's birth and death. People wallow in their unproductive minds. They get entangled in a web of imaginations far removed from reality. They may otherwise oscillate from the regrets of the past or the anxieties of the future. When people are not in situational awareness, they barely touch upon the present. Time flies and wasted lives can never be recovered.

Time cannot affect mindfulness, even though, the spirit of mindfulness rides on the temporal dimension. Any task has a start and end time. However, one does not look at mindfulness as an activity with a beginning or finish line. In fact, it glides along with any activity one engages with, at any moment. There are the intensity and quality associated with the task which makes it fresh any time, and every time one does it.

Imagine condensing ordinary matter out of energy: a case for spontaneous creation

When it comes to utilising material things, people are very unconscious in their extravagance. They dig up resources from the earth, burn holes in the air and pollute the water bodies to such an extent to make future life on the planet difficult. Sadly, they do not seem to realise the connection they have with matter and live responsibly. People exploit the planet so rapidly that it may go barren in a few centuries.

There is a chain of processes, which transform raw materials to the finished goods one uses. Does one ever take a step back to feel the transformation of matter that one holds? Being aware of this makes one sensitive to the link between humans and ecology. In that moment of honesty, one will value matter and will be in tune with nature.

For sustainability, people need to be more circumspect in the way they manage energy resources. The future of humanity and also many life forms depend on the friendly generation and utilisation of energy. Burning of fossil fuels only adds more woes to the fragile environment. The aim is to achieve 'energy freedom' in this century itself. Energy demands have soared by leaps and bounds. This is to cater to satisfy people's thirst for comfort and vanity.

Simple living is to be in contentment with local goods and services. That will hardly attract the heavy price one pays for an ecological collapse. If only people think twice before any action that drains energy, the world will be a better place. Mindfulness pauses one to be aware of the futility of sense gratification, *ad nauseum*. When the desire for sensual pleasures is minimal, one's consumption level also tapers down. Energy saved is energy retained for future generation.

How does meaning emerge out of signals?

Modern life brims with an overdose of signals from natural sources and manmade gadgets. It is smart to filter what is necessary and let go of the unwanted signals that one receive. Think of the ubiquitous cell-phone that disturbs one in the middle of a meeting. The internet too provides an information overload. Clarity helps one in not getting addicted to unproductive hyper-linkages. Objective use of information leads to a better filter that charges one's conditioning. Data is free in the modern age. Therefore, one needs discretion in its use. Mindfulness makes people non-judgmental about the information they process.

Signals are magic; one's impressions decide what one does with the input.

Social networking sites are not just hubs of information exchange. They offer space for everyone to strip their minds and post their thoughts moment to moment. It is good to make one's voice heard. However, the cacophony of voices, most often, makes these sites into noisy outposts signifying nothing. It is therefore, all the more important for people not to be carried away by such mindless data floating adrift in the cyberspace. Mindfulness brings back the focus one very much needs to sift information from data, in such a sea of signals.

Destroy the environment: mass suicide made easy

An energy field bathes the earth for life to function. There is a protective layer around the earth to filter out harmful radiations from space. Industrialisation and carbon emissions puncture this sheath. It will be in humanity's peril if people do not set this natural armour right. There is only lip service for the proactive steps needed to turn around the damage. Despite facts and figures of the looming calamity, no nation shows any commitment, to change.

Ownership counts a lot in environment. Normally, people hold views in the following way. "I own my house, so I take care of it. I love my family, so I take care of them. I need not take care of the things I do not own." Only when there is a connection to something, there is ownership. Quite often, even knowledge and experience fail to change attitudes. Environmental issue is one such example. The pressing question is how to break the impasse.

Environmental awareness can brighten up the future of life on earth. Today's collective failure need not be the final word. Action based on unconditioned mind is fresh and intense. The movement of such a society will be the antidote to the chaos and divisions seen in the world. It is for everyone to reckon the ways and means to do it. The inertia that stifles change is the conditioning people carry. They need to open up channels for jettisoning their old habits.

People claim progress often sacrificing clean air, pure water and functioning sanitation. Unpolluted air is a luxury for billions of people. It is a shame that one lives in cities blanketed with toxic fumes, smoke and dust. Forget the stench of garbage and filth strewn all over the streets. The world needs to usher in a better environment. An excellent balance between progress and cleanliness is the way forward. Realising the urgency to know oneself and engaging with the world consciously will be a decent start. Vandalising the environment directly or indirectly will then feel like injuring oneself.

Awareness of awareness of awareness . . . Is one situated between parallel mirrors?

Self-awareness, or the ability to be aware of one's own awareness, is a huge evolutionary leap. Awareness lets one look at the play of other faculties in consciousness. Thanks to this mysterious faculty, the universe becomes cognisable. Most often people identify themselves with their impressions. They tend to lose touch with reality, and their situational awareness suffers a lot. Grounding in one's own awareness leads one aside from the distractions of the mind. Mindfulness or meditation happens when one is in reality, and not carried away by imagination. Awareness opens up possibilities to step back and watch oneself and the world anytime. Reflecting on this faculty and experiencing its nature is taking the journey of self-discovery in the right direction.

The Form

Breath is movement. Life is movement. Mindfulness is in the movement.

One can practice mindfulness either at rest or while moving. That includes walking, talking, eating or engaging in any other activity. For instance, during walking; the gait, the muscles, the arm-swing, the speed and many things that go with the walk could be one's focus. Similarly, one can be conscious of the various sub-movements that add up to a main activity.

Breathing is an activity that happens from birth to death without one's need for attention. It is involuntary and air is the basis for life. The breath bridges the body and mind by bringing focus and settling emotions. Pranayama is an ancient yogic practice of conscious breathing. There is a very calming effect, apart from clearing the passage-way of one's lungs. Rhythmic breathing works on a set ratio of inhalation, retention and exhalation. It is advisable to take a few sessions of training from a qualified yoga instructor before practising it regularly.

Scientific studies have confirmed the positive effect of de-stressing the body and mind through deep breathing. The latest studies have confirmed that breath analysis is a stress detection tool. There are several other bio-markers that can be studied through breath profiling. Diseases like multiple cancers, asthma and even tuberculosis can be tested using such methods. Mindfulness of breathing is well worth the practice. Try out a basic breathing exercise now.

Sit comfortably with the spine erect, if possible, and relax. Watch the breathing patterns. Be conscious of the way air gushes in and fills the lungs. Then feel the force with which it comes out taking all the toxins the lung membranes have exchanged with pure oxygen. Sometimes, air enters through one nostril and leaves through the other. It removes the blocks if any in this life nourishing process. One could feel even the tip of the nose and upper lip quiver when the air is cold. Watchfulness reveals the many factors involved in breathing.

Do not sensationalise sensations.

The mind normally wanders, but when one focuses on the task one does, there is attention. When one starts witnessing, it sublimates hidden things to the surface of one's consciousness. The sensations from the respective organs can be ready subjects for mindfulness. This habit may trigger attention to all one does. With less distraction, there is more efficiency in one's endeavours. In fact, people can be more creative with their lives through mindfulness. Watching mental chatter is another technique that is effective in quietening the mind. Situational awareness is mindfulness when one engages with the world.

The blind see if only people will their eyes.

Vision is a pre-eminent gift to understand the nature and life. The light energy propagates as electromagnetic waves. It gets reflected from an object and passes through the eyes into the brain for processing. Images form as patterns of neuro-chemicals, and one perceives the world. Humans can also differentiate millions of colours thanks to the rods and cones in their eyes. Awareness makes one see the colours and forms of the world.

People who appreciate the beauty in nature may love the way light changes its hues at dusk and dawn. It is so mesmerising and relaxing to watch the ocean changing its colour depending upon the mood of the weather. Even mundane things like the shades of walls, floors, trees, have many colourful tales to tell. Be conscious of the eyes bathing in the sea of colours every moment. Language has limitations when it comes to sharing one's innermost thoughts or forms. The colour red, one thinks of, need not be the red that another mentions. Experiencing and being aware of what one sees is mindfulness in action.

There are no ear-lids. One may go on a noise diet.

Sound can be music, speech or plain noise. Life without any sound at all will be a dull world. Sound is the main means of communication; its place in the list is before the written word. Speech comes straight from the heart. More importantly there is an identity to every speaker—a voice signature.

There are three factors that make sound definable. They are volume, frequency and harmonics. Amplitude of the sound wave or the volume gives loudness to it. Frequency or in normal parlance, the pitch gives the sound shrillness. The harmonics or the quality creates the distinction between two sound sources say a veena and a flute appear different for the same tune and loudness. These three factors define any sound wave.

When one listens intently to anyone speaking, focus will be on the texture and tone of the sound. The sound vibrates within the head for a moment before the meaning forms. There is already a storehouse of meaning in memory. People derive meaning out of the sounds they hear. Listening is the mindfulness of sound. People can avoid impulsive judgments by doing so. When people start listening to themselves, they will communicate better.

Sony Walkman revolutionised the way people listened to music. Music has become constant companions for people throughout the day; they listen to it whether they are at the wheels or even at work. The overload could cause injury to one's ears, and distraction to one's activity.

Additionally, there is a lot of emotional churning up that happens with different genres of music. Can one make silence, music to one's ears?

A person of good taste goes after healthy food.

The foods we eat produce the sensation of taste. It is so easy to be mindful of the food one takes. First, look at the food in hand. Feel it before and after taking it to one's mouth. Get the taste of the food and focus on it. There are six primary tastes, which are bitterness, saltiness, sourness, sweetness, savoury or umami (cheese) and piquancy (chilli, ginger). Just like primary colours can combine to create other colours, these six primary tastes combine to provide different tastes for the food. One could try this simple experiment to know these ingredients. Take a few grains of sugar and salt, a few drops of lemon juice, a single neem leaf, a lump of cheese or papad and one small piece of ginger. Try tasting these primary tastes one by one; first of all, feel them in the mouth. Be very watchful and be aware of the sensation of taste rising in the mouth.

People, in their hurry read or watch television, while eating. Most often, they are hardly aware of taste and texture of the food in their mouth. Eat slowly, attentively and start enjoying food. There is a huge difference in the way one treats food by being mindful of it. Dieters too can see a difference in their cravings getting reduced. Everyone benefits by choosing healthy food and relishing it.

Fragrance and bad odour: are they acquired sensations?

Having a nose for smell is a passport to tickle one's emotions and well being. Some people are allergic to strong smells. One can be mindful of this sensation, which has helped in evolution by rejecting stale and dangerous food. In modern times, people have to be reminded of this important sensation they possess. Addictives, like tobacco and hard liquor, rob one off the pleasures of what a delicate aroma can evoke. Being mindful of various smells can add one more dimension to one's sense of reality.

Do not be a touch-me-not.

There is a pathetic manifestation of advanced leprosy. The patients tend to lose the sense of touch. Imagine when one cannot feel anything at all. Whether it is hot or cold, soft or hard; nothing makes sense to the body. A hug or a kiss will not feel anything. Losing the sensation of touch is the worst consequence of leprosy.

The lucky people who have the tactile sensation intact can be mindful of touch. Touch and feel, all the contacts one makes. Hold, squeeze and play with the object and examine with total attention. Try silk, sandpaper, metal, wood and other materials.

Mindfulness makes one's life richer. Since, sensations are the data that one gets from the environment, being attentive to them brings more clarity. This attitude turns into one's nature and brings calmness and peace in one's engagement with life.

The Baggage one carries is nothing. Not knowing it clearly is everything.

The flowering of wisdom is a consequence of newer knowledge, the experience of being and awareness of one's conditioning. This understanding is a choice for everyone. Freedom from the ideas of realisation is imperative to exercise the choice of living in clarity. It is easy to get caught up in the folds of religion, culture, gender, nationality, language or even the impressions one acquires. Many people think of self realisation as a culmination of their identification with a religion or path. The difficulty to freeing themselves will be intense if they hold on to their positions strongly.

Clarify the constant interplay of impressions in one's mind. It helps in better understanding of one's own capabilities. One can also see the frailty of one's mental compass in conditioning the unknown as the primal object. The ensuing transparency, leads one to erase false ideas about oneself, and fantasies about what one should be. In short, it liberates one to accept life in celebration. Doubts persist as to whether; knowledge on realisation or experiencing an epiphany is *moksha*. For many, realisation is a goal to achieve, through *sadhana*. In this text, realisation is not an object. There is no path to obtain the object, either.

The urge to know is innate in everyone. It gets satisfied through one's living experiences, and knowledge gained. The quest to know the laws of nature gets satiated through science. People express themselves through art. These have nourished the human development. The key to an evolved world is in the hands of the people. The trick is in adapting to one's impressions without being intolerant. The rigidity is in the inertia of losing in one's conditioning.

Conditioning through the millennia has invariably made people hold on to culture and tradition often unquestioningly. They lead their lives pacifying themselves in crisis or thanking the stars in better times. It is never late to look critically at one's impressions—knowledge, experience and conditioning. This is not to suggest, even for a moment, to discard or suppress them in any manner. People shall be better off having a reality-check on the nooks and corners of their own minds. It is enjoyable and will bring about many serendipitous discoveries on the way.

Objectivity with knowledge delivers.

People flounder in an existential whirlpool when there is no clarity in their thinking. Clarity brings in objectivity and vice versa. Objectivity is like a sword that cuts through the cerebral cobwebs of fancies and fantasies. This is not a chicken and egg story. One realises when one is objective in life. However, the big question is, how does one remain objective in times of extreme turmoil?

When one loses reason for passion, regrets cloud over one's past actions, and anxieties create fear about the future. Without clarity, any decision today may lead to bitterness tomorrow. At the same time, there is no point in evaluating whether one is objective or not. By doing so, there is stress, and one slips into being very self-judgmental.

Objectivity applies the spurs to pure action. Being conscious is basic to turn subjectivity to objectivity. The choice for freedom and clarity lies with everyone at every moment. Sadly, due to the enormous conditioning and fundamentalist beliefs entrenched in most of the people, clarity is the casualty. It becomes trapped deep within one's consciousness.

Observe the mind closely and one can see the difference. Freedom does not come easy. It is a constant endeavour to be on watch and catch irrational ideas taking hold of one's mind and personality. In fact, it is easy to be a fundamentalist or a bigot. This need not be in religion alone. The same attitude can spill over into other facets of life, as well. Mindfulness or witnessing the consciousness sans bias needs courage.

There is no examiner to grade one's action as objective or irrational. The proof of the pudding lies in the eating. A simple reality check is the peace and contentment in life irrespective of one's given situation. This is not to make a comparison in checking who is more objective than the other in any situation. This is not a skill either. Being in clarity is its own reward and is effortless.

Everyone is unique. People lose their individuality if they follow others blindly. Objectivity breaks the bondage people carry unknowingly. It makes one free and fearless and turns one's attention impartially to things on hand. Objectivity illuminates the consciousness to cut through the maelstrom of conditioning people hold on to unconsciously. The resulting courage is not out of selfishness or in being head strong. It is to stand on ones true nature and live accordingly with no regrets. It is pure action and may even be a trailblazer in the vast possibilities of social intercourse.

THE FUTURE PERFECT

Que cera, cera. Control the future. Be indifferent, and mind your own life. God made the world. He knows what to do. It is time to live literally as said in the scriptures. No god. Androids will rule the future. What change does one envisage? Life will go on with just cosmetic changes. The world will end soon. Hope they conquer death, so that, one can live forever. Future is unknowable. Work gives way for more leisure. Why worry; death takes care of the individual, and humanity will soon destroy itself. Heaven can be brought to earth, if only . . .

Call the astrologer. No, call the physicist.

The philosopher is dead.

Why not implore the priest? They repeat the scriptural prophecies like an imposition.

Who knows the future? Well, who can know it?

Good-bye to the future. Freedom at last!

Does life have a beginning or an end? It all depends on what framework one looks into the question. In a very narrow sense, existence ends with one's death. From a larger perspective, life has been manifesting for ages. Similarly, self-realisation is not a mile stone for people to reach and then thump their chest proclaiming victory. It is conscious impassionate attention, which is natural with anyone at anytime.

The world is in the throes of sorrow and violence in an unprecedented scale. How can the world feed the need, greed and desires of the billions of people? Mere material development does no justice in this quest. The quality of life naturally dips, and there can only be more suffering. In the same breath, if individuals enlighten their consciousness, there can be a collective surge in understanding and evolution.

There is a way out of the quagmire for the humans. People believe that a chance for the self to escape bondage and privation in this existence is through self-realisation. It is a prescription for the individual to get a ticket to heaven. However, society needs billions out of the loop quickly so that a chain reaction can make the world better. It is simple, even though, the problems seem very daunting and formidable. What is the way forward in raising quality of lives?

In retrospect, throughout history religious figures have been clamouring for individual salvation. The leaders, as well as, their followers claim that it could be achieved either now or after death, through certain prescribed rites. The pivot on which this rests is the unknown, which no one knows for sure. As a result, there are irreconcilable divisions among the peoples of the world.

To the question in hand, collective evolution is not in proselytising any sectarian values or ideas. On the contrary, it is about egging on people to taking responsibility of their own selves. It does not depend on the unknown, but very much rooted in the known. That makes the whole process tangible, rational and common for everyone. This secular approach to freedom and understanding can be easily brought home to people. Reinventing oneself is in letting go of the past. Evolution nurtures a climate of openness where everyone has the chance to live in objectivity.

Imagine after Armageddon, a group of hundred thousand people are stranded on an island. How can they fashion a community out of this motley crowd? For this inchoative experiment to mature, the spirit of self-discovery can offer many insights. One can consider even the present society as a case in point and work towards collective evolution. People need not wait for any national calamity, to prepare themselves to engage objectively with their society.

Self-discovery is not in escaping situations and synthesising an idealistic life based on various philosophies or traditions. It is not in evangelising religion or any idealism unilaterally, either. Understanding one's life processes is so simple and natural. Life exists in its rawness, mystery, variety, and independence to make a sensitive person seek for self-knowledge. When the seeking subsides, there is space for peace and a chance to live in full attention and totality.

One need not become a hermit to feel a contrived peace in isolation. On the contrary, one can engage in the world with all its problems and pleasures. A life for discovery is simple, yet effective. Live and let live; understanding collective advancement is a step away when people start discovering themselves and live in freedom.

An 'I' for a future perfect world

Self-discovery connotes individual centric action. It encourages one to understand and act in harmony with oneself and the world. Just like individuals, the world too has a consciousness of its own. It is an evolving template of ideas and aspirations, which can be described in relation to past observations. This collective movement propels humanity towards a future which, strangely cannot be predicted with certainty. It is as clear as an individual's future in these times of rapid change. It may be another story, had there been a homogeneous population with less variation among the people. Then, the individual and collective consciousness might have moved in step with each other.

From the dawn of civilisation, humanity has been fighting for survival; it still does. Social organisation came in later; it is work in progress. The last couple of centuries saw tremendous growth through science and technology. There are still vast swathes of population untouched by modernity. However, now people do have at least a rough idea of how the other half lives. This fuels desire for the have-not to acquire comforts to match with the luckier ones. The world calls this progress. This gargantuan motion of the collective mind has been set apace to give wings to the dreams of the many in their lifetime itself. From science to commerce, all the social institutions are in full swing to achieve this.

People want instantaneous fructification of their desires. When one tries to condense time, one must be prepared for lots of friction along the way. The world is witness to rapid rise in the economies of many nations. The greed and bitterness manifest in actual wars and protectionism to settle scores among themselves. Ideologies and identifications force them to push their own agenda among the weaker societies. The fractured world does not move as one entity. There are many differences among them, which push and pull the world in disunity. As a consequence, the overall growth is stunted. On reflection, this is the predicament of the world.

The dark side of society coexists with the brighter side of cooperation and growth. People are at different levels of development and abilities. It will not be fair to castigate a group or nation for the combined failures around the world. One observation stands out clearly; the weight of collective inertia pulls down even the few who aspire to rise above the mundane ordinariness of everyday life. It requires enormous grit and determination for anyone to overcome societal conditioning. The courage stems from an objective understanding of one's place in society. Self-discovery opens up the doors to know one's wants and duties in life.

Education, not necessarily in class rooms or institutions, can encourage critical thinking in society. It can offset the terrible indifference of people. This laid-back attitude, which is selfish in nature, adds on to the momentum of mass consciousness, which dissipates the collective energies of humanity. Once the apathy is removed or known, there will be a response from individuals to situations, which can pull society forward. Again, the definition of real progress is highly contentious with so many disparate groups lobbying for supremacy over the world.

Individuals make up the world, and it is in the fitness of things to expect all of them to know their place in society. When people have better awareness of themselves, there will be consensus and dialogue for conflict resolution. The movement of humanity, albeit non-linear in its direction has vitality and resilience in its manifestation. One can see the passion and emotions spilling over to defend their religion, nation or race. If only they read these wild emotions logically and calmly, there can be better outcomes to situations around the world. Knowing oneself lays bare the method to the madness one pursues blindly while following a conditioned script. Enlightened action follows once people discover themselves but planning anything before that, is again an emotional mind in work.

Future is in time, and perfection is in ideas. People often see their hopes crash severely even if they yearned for them. The fundamental necessity for anyone and any society is peace born of understanding. The world cannot be sane to traverse the path of death and destruction by the name of control and superiority. It cannot call itself progressive if it runs on an artificial thrust of pent-up mass conditioning, either. Sooner rather than later it will go back to instability.

There needs to be awareness among people to lead their lives based on authentic self-discovery. Humanity can then look forward to a world of greater tolerance and acceptance. The time and energy of the people can be well spent, and not be fizzled out in the usual violence and apathy. The mighty collective consciousness then pulls along individuals, left on the way, in its intrepid journey to the unknown future. A future perfect world starts now, and it starts with everyone.

Self-Discovery and the Collective Consciousness

"What one thinks is what one gets": everyone wants to achieve that. Man imagines landing on the moon. People fantasise about it, do the science and finally reach there. Discovery after discovery of the secrets of nature has opened the doors for many such impossible dreams to take wings. The seeds of destruction, nevertheless, come along with this motto since everyone needs to think alike.

There is indeed collective consciousness in operation. One such proof is the industrial revolution in Europe, which nurtured the flowering of the greatest scientific minds; the world has ever seen. It did not happen in some other part of the world. Similarly, the trinities in Carnatic music were contemporaries who were born in and around Thanjavur. One cannot expect the geniuses to be born in another continent or time, far removed from the culture that promoted this type of music.

The present consciousness has all the ingredients to encourage material greed, innovative spirit, faster transportation and communication, greater individual freedom, and in general, a continuation of the trajectory of growth of the past centuries. At the same time, it is besotted with cries of tribalism, religious fundamentalism, jingoistic nationalism, misogynist attitudes and indifference masquerading as right conduct. The sheer heterogeneous nature in the world and its people present a dichotomous picture of growth and stagnation.

The future beckons both the mindsets in an equal measure. One group is, by and large, ready to experience the brave new world. The other group fears to let go of the glorified past deeply entrenched in them. Even the people, who hold on to their conditioned beliefs as sacrosanct, have one thing in common. They make use of all the comforts that the world can offer. What is right and what is wrong is not for anyone to say. Nevertheless, one can witness the way one's mind works and take decisions in clarity.

Tantalising opportunities may unsettle some, whereas, others may withdraw to teleological succour in their engagement with change. Future, if at all one is alive, is again an opportunity to witness, and act from one's impressions. There may be additional knowledge to support newfound experiences, but is one really free of one's conditioning to embrace life in totality?

Self-discovery allows one to face any situation neither from the anxiety of gaining nor from the fear of losing something. Mass consciousness evolves with increasingly unbiased individual action. One feeds on the other; self-discovery and the collective consciousness can tango for eternity. Future holds promise for many concerted breakthroughs in science, and also humanity to progress in freedom. Self-discovery is the key for individuals to realise themselves and let the world evolve.